BE MONEY SMART IN TOUGH TIMES

FOR PARENTS & GRANDPARENTS

NEALE S. GODFREY

Johnson —
Happy Money !
XO, Neale

Published by GreenStreet Commons, Inc.
Sparta, New Jersey

Copyright © 2021 by GreenStreet Commons, Inc.

All rights reserved, including the right of reproduction in whole or in part in any form.

In accordance with the U.S. Copyright Act of 1976, the scanning, uploading, and electronic sharing of any part of this book without the permission of the publisher constitute unlawful piracy and theft of the author's intellectual property. If you would like to use material from the book (other than for review purposes), prior written permission must be obtained by contacting Neale Godfrey at neale@nealegodfrey.com.

GreenStreet Commons, Inc.
c/o Neale Godfrey
11 Laurel Terrace
Sparta, NJ 07871

www.nealegodfrey.com

Printed in the United States of America

First Edition: March 2021
10 9 8 7 6 5 4 3 2 1

Library of Congress: 2020917981

Other Titles by Neale Godfrey

- *New York Times #1 Best Seller; Money Doesn't Grow on Trees: A Parent's Guide to Raising Financially Responsible Children*
- *National Best Seller; A Penny Saved: Teaching Your Children The Values and Life Skills They Will Need to Live in The Real World*
- *From Cradle to College [AND EVERYTHING IN BETWEEN]: A Parent's Guide to Financing Your Child's Life*
- *MAKING CHANGE: A Women's Guide to Designing Her Financial Future*
- *MOM, INC.: Taking Your Work Skills Home*
- *The Kids' Money Book*
- *Neale Godfrey's Ultimate Kids' Money Book*
- *Why Money Was Invented*
- *Why Money Was Invented - Teacher's Guide*
- *Here's The Scoop: Follow An Ice Cream Cone Around The World*
- *Here's The Scoop: Follow An Ice Cream Cone Around The World - Teacher's Guide*
- *A Money Adventure: Earning, Saving, Spending and Sharing*
- *A Money Adventure : Earning, Saving, Spending and Sharing - Teacher's Guide*
- *From Beads to Banknotes: The Story of Money*
- *From Beads to Banknotes: The Story of Money – Teacher's Guide*
- *From Beads to Banknotes: The Story of Money – Learning Masters*
- *Check It Out: The Book About Banking*
- *Check It Out: The Book About Banking – Teacher's Guide*
- *Check It Out: The Book About Banking – Learning Masters*
- *Taking Stock: The World of Business*
- *Taking Stock: The World of Business – Teacher's Guide*
- *Taking Stock: The World of Business – Learning Masters*
- *Life Inc.: The Ultimate Career Guide for Young People*
- *Life Inc.: The Ultimate Career Guide for Young People – Teacher's Guide*
- *Life Inc.: The Ultimate Career Guide for Young People – Student Journal*
- *The Eco-Effect: The Greening of Money*
- *Money Town – CD Rom*
- *Neale Godfrey's Green$treets Activity Book*
- *Green$treets: Unleash The Loot! (#1 Educational Gaming app)*
- *Green$treets: Shmootz Happens! (iOS Educational Gaming App)*
- *Green$treets: Heifer International (iOS Educational Gaming App)*

To Gavin and Bodhi

You are the most kind, smart, empathetic, funny and loving people I know. You both are the Super Heroes who can change the world. You have learned what you live and I know that you will grow up to live what you have learned.

My Mom, Georgine said to me when I gave birth to my children; "You will never know how much you can love someone until you have a child." She was right, but she didn't prepare me for having grandchildren. I thought I knew what love was...and then along came my grandchildren; Gavin and Bodhi.

My grandchildren are part of the family chain of love that has connected us through the generations; from past to future: from my Great Grandma Molly and Grandpa Jake to Grandma Jewel and Grandpa Bill and Ady and Doonie; to My Mom, Georgine. The links of our family chain are strong...we may add to them, but the bonds between my grandchildren will never break. They offer me unconditional love, pride and joy.

I dedicate my book to you both; Gavin and Bodhi. You are my soccerist-playing, Tik-Tokingist, crazy-adventurists who see all the possibilities in life that I can't even dream of. Thank you for blessing me with my title of; Grandma Neale. I can't wait to continue our time; laughing, living and most of all...of loving each other.

Acknowledgement

There is one person who has committed tireless advice, counsel, wisdom and grunt-work to make this book happen. Jesse Broome is that person. He has been my wonderful and loyal; Sancho Panza; Robin; and Igor.

Jesse always remains calm in the midst of my storm and stays laser-focused on the trees when I get lost in the forest.

Thank you, Jesse.

"Neale Godfrey's **Be Money Smart in Tough Times: For Parents and Grandparents** is not only a must-have guide for parents and grandparents but for every adult to understand their relationship with money. It is an incredible tool for teaching financial literacy to children of all ages, even the adult kids, but it also teaches values and responsibility. It gives parents a clear-eyed view of their financial acumen and also helps them understand when they are using money as a substitute for something else in their relationship with their kids. This is a book about life, it is just taught through the lens of money."

Joyce M. Roché
former President and Chief Executive Officer
of Girls Incorporated

———

"Raising financially-smart kids from a young age is imperative as it gives them the financial building blocks to better prepare them for their future. The earlier that parents teach their kids about personal finance, the more time their kids will have to learn, ask questions, and make mistakes in a safe and supervised way. Neale's work in the financial literacy space is so important, and this book will be a great resource for all families as they raise the next financially successful generation."

Tim Sheehan
Co-Founder and CEO of Greenlight

———

"Financial literacy and empowerment is a community obligation. This book is a must-read and packed with the ideas, lessons, and tools we all need to hear to help build the brightest financial future for the next generation."

Caleb Frankel
Co-Founder & COO, EarlyBird

"My Secure Advantage performs educational Money Coaching sessions with thousands of employees every month. Sadly, there is one common denominator which is that Americans are thrown into adulthood completely unprepared to navigate the complexities of life's financial journey. Knowledge of personal finance is the leading cause of stress in America. This dilemma transcends all socio-economic and generational classifications. **Be Money Smart in Tough Times** is exactly what we, as parents and grandparents, need to ignite an enthusiastic interest in this crucial topic that will lead to a lifelong positive impact for the next generation."

Brad Barron
CEO of My Secure Advantage

"As a CPA and a mother of three daughters, I was pleasantly surprised with the number of examples and exercises Neale had in this book. Her book helped me realize there were still many concepts and discussions around "money as a life skill" that I still needed to have with my kids. Whether you are a new parent or a grandparent, you will be guided on how to work her four-jar system with different sections tailored to different age groups. From coin identification games for the little ones to set up a lease with your adult child, her book has something for everyone. She takes the often-complicated topic of money and simplifies it around the concept of Earning, Spending, Saving, and Sharing. I will definitely be recommending this book to all my friends that have kids! Thank you, Neale."

Shaun Budnik
Past President, Deloitte Foundation
Retired Partner, Deloitte LLP, and KPMG US

Summary

These times are unprecedented. You may have become sick; lost loved ones; lost your job; lost your ability to even go out to dinner. Your kids and grandkids are homeschooling and distancing. And, this is a time to either fall apart emotionally and financially or ban together as a family and community. Either way, we must move forward to the "new normal." We have no idea what that means, but we also know this is going to go on for a while. So, I want to be your mentor through this process and help you and your kids and grandkids to be financially resilient in these tough times.

As my business colleague and friend, Mike Hackett, SVP of My Secure Advantage has said, "In these times we can either break down or break through. It is our choice." This book will help you and your family to "break through". We are resilient and adaptive, and we need to muster all of our strength now for ourselves and for the next generation. We not only need to adapt with each other, we need to adapt for each other. Together, we can do this. We have seen courage and sadness and hope. Maya Angelou said it best; "I can be changed by what happens to me. But I refuse to be reduced by it."

Before this all happened and if you are a parent or a grand-parent you might have worried that you could be raising a spoiled or entitled child. That could still be the case, but it seems like a long time ago that that was a worry. We all want to be good parents. We all want our kids to grow up with a healthy attitude toward money, so that someday they can leave the nest and make it on their own. Well, lots of us have blown it and we hear our little ones whine for what they want; we hear our teens say, "I'll be ruined if I don't get what I want;" and we see our adult children coming home to live in, "Hotel Mom and Dad" (replete with room service and gas in the car). These issues will still be part of our consciousness and will be issues that we will face. If any of this resonates with you, help is here.

Neale Godfrey, the creator of the topic of "Kids and Money" in the 1980s when she feared that her children were suffering from the "I want, I want syndrome," is here to help you every step-of-the way. You may have read one of Neale's 27 books or have seen her on one of 13 appearances on Oprah or other TV shows, or your kids may have used her financial literacy curricula in school or after school. Neale Godfrey is the definitive voice for teaching financial responsibility, and her expertise will help you and your kids (of any age) grow up to be economically independent and achieve their financial dreams.

Introduction

Even in these tough times, when we are so distracted, we need to keep parenting. And it's more important than ever to make sure that we are the parents we want to be. Why? Because if we don't set our kids up for success, we set them up for failure.

You may not have raised your kids to be financially responsible. Maybe you never taught them the basic money facts-of-life so they could have the money *mo-jo* to live and thrive on their own someday. You may have supported the "I want, I want" syndrome. You doled out a $20 here and a $20 there, because, "Hey, they are just kids." And you picked up the tab as they grew up and allowed them to think that, indeed "Money <u>Did</u> Grow On Trees." You allowed grandma and grandpa to spoil them. You handed them one of your credit cards as they went to the mall and later to college. You didn't make them get "side" jobs to earn money. And, you allowed them to move back into "Hotel Mom and Dad" when they should have left the nest to experience the financial facts of life all on their own. By the way, you even allowed Hotel Mom and Dad to come complete with room and laundry service and gas in the car. Co-dependence and financial illiteracy follow our kids into adulthood.

In our Post-COVID-19 world all of these facts will have changed. They have gotten worse, with lay-offs and kids graduating from college only to see internships dry up and prospects for jobs they were educated for disappear. Many of our recent grads say that their college education was a waste of time and money. They have taken on debt. Their parents are most likely among the furloughed or laid-off workers who are really scared about the future. Most people in our country have to borrow to even cover a $400 emergency. We were not prepared for this crisis. The country was not ready; our leadership was not ready; and individuals were not ready.

I'm turning the clock back so you can look at the statistics of Pre-COVID-19, so that you can start to examine your past. You will now get to do a "Pause" and "Reset." But you need to know where you have been before you can change how you want to go forward.

Facts:

- Each year, the financial literacy of America's youth continues to decline. According to the Council for Economic Education, fewer than 17% of the graduating class of 2019 were required to take one semester of personal finance classes.
- In a 2017 study conducted by Financial Engines,[1] only "six percent... were able to pass a quiz about a broad range of financial decisions they most likely will need to make during their lives."
- *Our kids have flunked a basic financial literacy test.* Our kids answered 58% of the questions correctly, according to National Financial Educators Council, 2018.[2]
- *The average student loan debt for 2020 was over $35,000,* according to Student Loan Planner.[3] There are approximately 43 million student borrowers and almost 3 million of them owe $100,000 or more. About 92% of student loans are federal. The average monthly student loan payment is almost $400 per month. (Note: It would cost a person about $530 a month to carry a $100,000 30-year mortgage at 5% interest.) And, the average student loan delinquency rate was over 11%, pre-COVID-19. That is really bad when you put it in perspective, that for the first quarter of 2020, all consumer loans had a delinquency rate of 2.47%, according to the Federal Reserve.[4]

- *55% of parents have more than $40,000 in student debt,* according to StudentLoanHero.com.[5] Parents borrowed approximately $36,000 under the Federal Parent PLUS[6] program.
- *Your children are either not leaving the nest or coming back home... and you are picking up the bill.* According to Pew Research Center,[7] "For the first time in more than 130 years, Americans ages 18-34 are more likely to live with their parents than in any other living situation." We don't know the effect of this now in our era of the Pandemic and post-Pandemic. I expect a lot more Gen-Zers will return home because they can't find jobs.

Does this financial literacy follow our kids into adulthood? The answer is a resounding: Yes.

Pre-COVID-19, in 2019, total consumer debt in our country was $14.1 trillion dollars,[8] or an average of personal debt of over $90,000 per household. The numbers during our pandemic have already been increasing. During the first quarter of 2020, household debt increased by almost $200 billion, and rising.

The dust has not settled yet on the financial effects of the pandemic. But we do know that unemployment rose to upwards of 20% (Depression levels) and according to a new 2020 study on the workplace, Capital One[9] and The Decision Lab found that "77% of respondents noted that they felt anxious about their financial situation, with 58% feeling that finances control their lives." The National Endowment for Financial Education[10] has released data stating, "Nearly 9 in 10 say that the COVID-19 crisis is causing financial stress." People have not saved enough for emergencies or retirement.

My Secure Advantage is on the front line, seeing this every day as they coach employees to take charge of their financial lives. Brad Barron, CEO told me that the one common denominator that his money coaches see with their clients is that "Adults are thrown into adulthood completely unprepared to navigate their money journey. We see this in the tragically high percentage of working Americans that are far from being on track to retire and have a lifestyle that is not impoverished. This is why personal finance is the leading cause of stress in America. This dilemma transcends all socio-economic and generational classifications."

Is this really the legacy we want to leave to our kids? The question we need to ask is "Why was all of this happening and why were you buying into not being prepared for our financial future and not preparing our kids for theirs?" Maybe it felt good to see your kids' faces light up temporarily when you showed up with that special gift? Perhaps you didn't have all these wonderful extras when you grew up, and you wanted your kids to have them now? Was it easier to substitute "stuff" for the "time" you didn't have to spend with them? Maybe you just wanted them to be kids and not to have to worry about money? Perhaps you felt that "polite people should not talk about money," so you hid the financial facts of life? Were you trying to "keep up with the Joneses" and to make sure that your kids had all of the cool possessions the other kids had? Maybe you didn't want your Ex to buy them that overindulgent gift to prove he was the "cool parent" and you preempted that purchase? Maybe you secretly took out your 401(k) money to write the check for college because you were so proud that your child got into that private school of their dreams and you didn't have the heart to explain that you just couldn't afford it without going into your retirement funds?

Don't beat yourself up. These are your kids; your kids are your heart. I get it. I have two kids and two grandkids. When

I had my kids over 30 years ago, my mother said, "You will never know how much you can love until you have a child." That is it. Full stop. We will do anything for our kids. We will sacrifice anything for them. We will give our kids the shirt off our backs. So, if we don't have clear boundaries around *Love* and *Money*, how can we convey our values to them? Of course, it's easier to sacrifice than to be the disciplinarian. It's way more fun to hear the squeals of delight than hear the constant whining that goes along with, "No." And, I'm not recommending too strict parenting. You don't want your home to be the prison, with you as the Warden. Your kids will just become angry and lose the joy of being kids. Your kids are going to remember the time with you, not what you spent on them. They will outgrow the outfits; the toys will break and become boring; the latest smart phone will suddenly become outdated, but your kids will never outgrow your love and devotion, which will never be measured in "stuff."

What does this mean? It means that not dealing with these money issues and allowing the "drip, drip," of money flowing out, and more importantly, your values going down the drain along with that money, does not help your kids; in the short or long term. It means that you may start depleting your retirement savings. It means that your kids can rake up huge college debt (along with you) and: **It means that you have encouraged your kids to "steal" your money.**

If any of this resonates with some of your behavior, I'm here to help, so keep reading. If none of this is you and you are confident that your offspring will be secure with the unexpected and expected curve-balls life is sure to throw at them financially...throw my book away. (Or better yet, give it to a parent or grandparent who is not as lucky as you.)

Why I Wrote This Book (and others)

I wrote this book because you have asked me to write it. I speak to parents and grandparents all of the time. I give presentations for corporations, public meetings, women's groups, military personnel (in some cases Wounded Vets), for college groups, financial houses, for school administrators, teachers, and children of all socio-economic levels, for the media on TV, radio, podcasts, webinars, social media... And the issues remain the same. We are all petrified that we are raising financially illiterate kids who will not be able to thrive on their own. We have failed as parents.

You may not have set the best example for your kids, and this may have become very obvious in these trying times. You are not alone. As I said before, many people have to borrow even to cover a $400 emergency. And in the pandemic, many people spent more online than they spent before. We called it Comfort Shopping and excused this behavior as a coping mechanism. Come on! You may not have a job... and your kids see your reaction to that by you shopping? Not only is this bad financial planning, but it also sends the wrong message to your kids. We all hoped that this wouldn't matter. But today, in our environment, when you may have been furloughed, or worse yet, laid-off, the emergency money is a need... and is really needed.

Even in these tough times, many parents are handing their credit cards to their kids to let them shop online or as they can go back into the malls. When I get in people's faces and say, "You are allowing your kids to manipulate you?" Rather than the pushback and the self-righteous and defensive response, I thought I'd get; I overwhelmingly hear, "I know, and I need help. Neale, help me."

I'm here to help; to share some life hacks about money. I am also as passionate about raising financially resilient children and grandchildren as I was when I started this journey in 1985 with my children. So, I wrote this book for all of you parents and grandparents who want to have a road map to raise money-savvy offspring, of any age. With a little coaching, you can press the "Pause Button" and start over from where you went off the rails. It is never too late. More importantly, it is never too early to start these lessons. I liken it to potty training. It's a life skill your kids will need. It's easier to start it when they are young. If you wait until your kids are in high school, it's a bigger and messier job!

I'm the guru in this field of teaching kids about money. I created the topic when my kids shocked me, as little ones, by being financially illiterate. I intervened and wrote the first book to help them and you. **Money Doesn't Grow On Trees: A Parent's Guide To Raising Financially Responsible Children** hit #1 on *The New York Times Best Seller's List*. Why? Because you care about raising happy and healthy children, who can build and achieve their financial dreams.

Okay, I got some help from Oprah. As an on-air expert for four and a half years, Oprah believed that this was an essential topic and that all parents had to get involved. She once said on air, "I'd have children just to do Neale's allowance system." Her comment validated my work and made me do my "Happy Dance," as my books flew off the shelves.

The issues today are just as relevant as when Oprah had her network show. There was one that struck me. It was in the "Big Hair" days in 1994, but this scene could play out today.

The first show was in November, and I was on air with two families who were rapidly becoming dysfunctional because of their inability to handle the money part of their life with their kids.

The audience latched on to this.

One couple had spent $2,500 on Christmas for their kids! Their holiday spending spree had put them into the hole for the rest of the year. It took them the full year to pay it back, only to gear up for the next Christmas.

The second couple mortgaged their future to build a new wing on their house as a fantasy play world for their kids, complete with a sound system, TV, computer, and refrigerator. The parents seemed to think it was the way it had to be. "I give them things because they're things I wish I had when I was a kid," said the mother of these two boys. "If it makes them happy, it makes me happy."

But were the kids happy? They seemed pleased, but not satisfied. Would giving them more gifts satisfy them? The other family had six children! And they echoed the same thought: "The kids would be a lot happier if they could have all of the things that their friends do...We've gone into debt to meet those needs."

But did the kids need all that? The parents said Yes...they felt their kids would not be popular without all of this stuff. Oprah's audience didn't think so. They were yelling from their seats and were downright hostile to these "spoiled, greedy" kids – and the other kids in the audience were just as hostile as the adults! Oprah asked me if I would work with them—put them on budgets, try to develop healthy spending and saving habits—for the kids and parents. The families agreed to work with me, and I spent four months coaching them via phone.

When I returned with them, on-air, the families and—the eight kids had turned themselves around. If they seemed like selfish, greedy little brats in the first show, now they were lovely! More than that, they felt better about themselves. I put them on my work-for-pay allowance system. If they didn't earn money for what they wanted, they couldn't whine for it and get it from their parents. They did stick to their budgets and felt it was a cool challenge to earn money. They offered to pool their resources for Christmas and not to have their parents go into debt. They even pitched in with the household chores and became responsible citizens of a newly accountable family.

The parents began to realize that "stuff" didn't make up for their childhood of deprivation; that it was never about the stuff. We can't teach our kids to build a shield of "stuff" to protect them from bullies, no matter how hard we try. Keeping up with the Joneses only means that the bar continually moves upwards because you are always going to meet more entitled Joneses. And it's not about the Joneses; it's about you.

I began to realize that, yes, the lessons of budgeting, the teachings of financial responsibility, and the experiences I write and speak about, do apply to life's other issues. Teaching your children and grandchildren about value was a sound basis for teaching them about the way the world works; and more importantly, your values.

In many ways, this book is an extension of those early days that were represented by my two Oprah families, whom I came to admire for their courage in admitting their problems in front of the 30 million people in Oprah's audience. Their perseverance in addressing those issues caused the change. I only gave them the tools to help. They did it.

Unfortunately, this story is as relevant today as it was then (and maybe more so) because the peer pressure and access to information are even more significant today. The issues are the same.

My book is for all of you who care about your kids and grandkids as much as I do. We never want them to confuse Net Worth with Self Worth.

Okay, I feel as if a bed of inspirational music should now come up. I'm positive that you are thinking, "Well, sure, Neale has done it with her kids...but she just went through life humming the inspirational music she wants us to listen to and doesn't know how tough it is for me and my situation."

It all started when I was the President of The First Women's Bank, and I was just divorced. (Did I mention that my husband left me in the hospital for another woman 18 hours after our son was born? Did I also mention that I was in active labor for 2.5 months and was held hostage in an Intensive Care Unit in a hospital...and my son was going to be born a mess? I was running the bank from the hospital and got permission for my 3-and-a-half-year-old daughter to visit. She thought it was my office. [Actually, all offices should have intravenous drips!])

Okay, you can see that I have no issues! After I put my Big Girl panties back on and got the divorce, I was back at the bank and watching women struggling to handle their money. They were accomplished in every area of their lives, but felt inadequate about managing their own money. It stemmed from lots of things, one was that in the dark ages, "women were not supposed to be involved with money;" "polite people didn't talk about money;" and "we were never taught anything about money when we were young."

Financial illiteracy is not okay, and I wasn't about to let my kids grow up without understanding basic economics. So, I schlepped my kids around to every bookstore in NYC in 1986, to find books to teach them about money. But the problem was that there were no books to teach kids about money. The topic didn't have a dedicated book on the shelf. The topic didn't exist.

Of course, my then three-year-old daughter said, "Rather than keep taking us to bookstores to find a book to teach us about money, Mommy, why don't you just write the book." She saw the look on my face that said. "Whoa, I know how to be a bank president, but I don't know how to write a book." After seeing the consternation on my face, her next quip with her arms, akimbo was, "Oh, you're scared?" Being the great, sophisticated mother I am, I crouched and established eye contact with my three-year-old and said, "No, I'm *not* scared." But of course, I was, I was way outside my comfort zone. But I put on my Big Girl Panties and wrote the book.

If we fast forward, this is still as much of a National Emergency today, as it was in then. Yes, a National Emergency! And our current crisis highlights this even more.

TABLE OF CONTENTS

SECTION I

SECTION II

SECTION III

SECTION I

WHY IS IT IMPORTANT TO RAISE FINANCIALLY RESPONSIBLE CHILDREN AND GRANDCHILDREN?

SMALL CHANGE

RAISING FINANCIALLY RESPONSIBLE CHILDREN AND GRANDCHILDREN

If you are a parent or a grandparent, you may think that this is a rhetorical question. In a lot of ways, it is. We want our loved ones to grow up knowing that they can be happy and self-sufficient while designing and living a stress-free life. An independent, money-savvy child is the wish of every parent and grandparent. The good news is that your desire can become a reality.

But sometimes life gets in the way, and there are barriers to all of our dreams and plans. Life recently has gotten in the way... big time. We can take a step back from this time and learn something from it so we can be prepared to respond differently the next time life throws us a smack-in-the-face. It sometimes takes a disaster to also reveal a social disaster; our current situation has shown that, as well. Turn these trying times into teaching times.

When I was a kid, I heard stories about when my grandfather, Grandpa Bill, lost his first wife and his 18-month-old baby boy in the 1918 flu epidemic. But that was a story about the old days. It certainly couldn't happen to us. How do you plan for a disaster? Can you? We can't stop natural disasters, but we can plan for some of the unexpected things that may happen; and teach or kids to, as well. Howard Ruff pointed out that "It wasn't raining when Noah built the Ark."

So, our lives have just been running along. Sure, we have been through recessions, lay-offs and illness. Have we learned from them? Have we saved for a rainy day? Have we raised resilient kids? Horrible things will happen to many of us, it's part of life, and we never know what that can be. The problem is that it seems that when one strikes, and we think it's really bad, we don't have to wait very long for the next one to put the previous one into perspective.

I'm guessing that you and I are alike. I was afraid that my kids and grandkids were going to be influenced by peers and the media and not grow up with my values. If I wasn't going to take this task on, who was? I wanted my kids to develop self-esteem, sound judgment, self-discipline, and the ability to take care of themselves. (Okay, I also wanted the pleasure of making it through the grocery store without my cart loaded with all the junk the kids found.)

The most significant gift I can give my kids and grandchildren is the gift to teach them to design and plan for their future. A well laid out and executed plan is the first essential step towards financial wellness. Your plan, plus trusted sound advice, will allow your loved ones to dream their dreams and then see them fulfilled. As Benjamin Franklin said, "By failing to prepare, you are preparing to fail." Unless you have goals and a roadmap to reach those goals, you will be meandering through life, and others may be making the decisions for you. I wanted to empower my kids to own their dreams and financial roadmap to achieve true financial wellness. I can help you to do that for your children and grandchildren, as well. Trust me; I appreciate that you have lots of competition for your time and money. I will make this journey with you to help your kids and grandkids to attain financial freedom.

By the way, I think Ben Franklin was also talking about preparing for tough times. These are tough times. They will go away, but we need to learn the lessons we hopefully should have learned about planning. Ben was a big believer in conveying your values to your kids. That is what I will attempt here.

WHAT KIDS DON'T KNOW
CAN HURT THEM

There's nothing that you use more than money. You have a constant day-to-day interaction with it that requires continual decision making. You're never *not* making financial decisions—and if you're not making them based on knowledge, you're making them based on ignorance. You can come to worship money too much if you don't know the real value of money. It's very tempting for kids to see the quick bucks, and flashy power displays all over the media. What kids don't know about money *can* hurt them. Bad financial habits in childhood can lead to worse problems when you're a grown-up. Too much debt can cripple a family. Accordiwng to San Diego family law firm, Wilkinson & Finkbeiner, LLP, every 13 seconds,[11] there is one divorce in America, or approximately nine divorces in the time it takes for a couple to recite their wedding vows (two minutes).

Over a 40-year period, 67 percent of marriages will terminate. Money issues remain as the top cause of stress[12] for Americans, and fighting over money[13] still ranks as one of the leading reasons for divorce. We know the problems. Debt can put you in a hole you'll never get out of—from watching your credit rating plummet to losing your home. If you don't know the value of money, you can get duped easily — it happens all of the time.

Teaching your kids to have a good grasp on the financial realities is one of the best ways of preparing them to deal with all the unexpected challenges life will send their way. Life isn't fair. We all know that, and yet, it's still a shock every time unfairness confronts us — we need to be solidly grounded so that we're not emotionally and financially devastated when life throws us a curveball.

Relationships with other people can also be connected to money. That doesn't mean money is more important than love or friendship, or that people can be bought or sold—just that it's always there and always an object lesson in fairness or unfairness. Money is part of the parent-child relationship, from pay for chores to clothing allowances to college tuition. And, we know that it is often a crucial part of partner relationships, for better or worse. Naturally, it's at the heart of the business or employer-employee relationships, and it figures in friendships, as well, from transactions as simple as; "Who pays for lunch?" to the sometimes-bewildering borrowing and lending that goes on between school-age kids and their friends. The first step in understanding what money does and doesn't do is teaching your children not to confuse self-worth with net worth. The one who dies with the most toys *doesn't* win.

MONEY IS A TOOL

Through years of working with children and grandchildren, working with money, raising my children to be financially responsible and helping my grandchildren to be money savvy, one insight became more apparent to me. The lessons of financial exchange can be applied to social exchange. You must deal with money every day in many ways, but money itself, will not make you happy. As Ben Franklin said, "Money never made a man happy yet, nor will it. The more a man has, the more he wants. Instead of filling a vacuum, it makes one."

Teaching children about money is not teaching about greed or teaching them to become soulless, grasping little Ebenezer Scrooges. Money is about values, about relationships, about choices, and about self-esteem. The same dollar that's used to buy worthless items can be given to charity. The whined-for candy bar, either given or withheld from the mysterious bottomless well of parent's or grandparent's pockets, can be earned money, allotted for a bicycle or college, and the spoiled (but ultimately helpless) child becomes an empowered partner in their own choices.

Money is always a social issue; it never exists in isolation. You can...

➤ Earn it.
➤ Save it.
➤ Spend it.
➤ Share it.

You can't get it alone; you have to make a social contract with someone else and then fulfill your end of that contract. You can't spend it alone; you have to go back into society and make decisions. If you have a finite amount of money, and you understand that you have a better chance of making those decisions based on a mature assessment of the value of things. You can save it alone, but that's an intermediate step—the period of quiet contemplation and self-examination that's a necessary part of any social exchange. Saving alone means that you have probably squirreled your money away under your mattress or in a piggy bank. It will not work for you, if you do. Giving it means understanding how much you can afford to share and then sharing it with a socially worthwhile cause of your choice. To give, someone has to receive; again, this is a social exchange. Whatever your purpose is, charitable giving returns to us a sense of self-worth and a sense of connection with the community and world.

You can get money in wicked ways—you can take it without permission. You can spend it in harmful ways, like spending your money on junk and spending more than you have. You can save it in bad ways, by hoarding it. You can even give it away in the wrong ways, if you are trying to buy popularity.

For better or worse, money is one connection; be it, for parents and grandparents with kids of any age; frankly, it is for anyone who has a child in their lives. If you know that a value structure is essential and you want to teach it to the children in your life, you aren't sure where to start or how to go about it... this book is for you.

It is hard to know where to start these days. We live in a wonderfully multicultural society, with different philosophies, rules, and generational values. Money is one of the few things we have in common—and more than that, it's so tangible. Everyone knows what it is and what it measures by its buying power. Even in today's digital world

of fiat currency, money – however invented and used – is measured by its buying power.

The basic rule, found throughout every culture, in one form or another, is "Do unto others as you would have them do unto you." We understand the phrase to be the *Golden Rule*—a rule as solid as gold. Like gold, it can be used as a measurement of human virtue, a measurement of values.

As I've lectured over the years, written 27 books and financial literacy curricula and taught courses to parents, grandparents, and kids about handling money, I've spent a lot of time thinking about the broader applications of these lessons. I know that they can be applied step-by-step. The first step means that parents or parents-to-be must first assess their money-handling profile. Next, parents must work with their children to teach them money as a life skill. And with that in place, they can use a system of financial responsibility as the basic structure for a value system of their own.

The book will focus on children of different ages. So, whether you have a young child or teen or young adult in your life, you can connect with both the philosophy behind the book and the practical steps you can take with your child or grandchild. If your child or grandchild is already older when you begin this program, there's no need to feel discouraged. Just start where you are comfortable and work your way forward. Remember, you could get a "do-over" when you become a grandparent. You may even discover that as a grandparent, you have more time on your hands to help your children and grandchildren with these valuable lessons.

Each chapter of the book will include theoretical and practical information. Each may consist of: worksheets, quizzes, and games to involve you and your offspring in the basics of financial responsibility.

DEFINE YOUR GOALS:
A LOOK IN THE MIRROR

Before you go any farther, it is time to take a step back and look at how you, your partner, or spouse handle money. The first lessons, and most important lessons that children learn, are from their parents, not from the media or peers—especially in an area that's as emotionally sensitive as our attitudes toward money. So, answer the questions on this worksheet and eventually in a quiz as honestly as you can, remembering that you're not going to be graded on it or held against some unrealistic standard of perfection—not that such a thing exists. No one will tweet your answers!

We grow up with ideas about money that we got from our parents, and we pass them on to our kids. We may not want to pass some of them on. They may have worked in our parents' generation, but they may no longer work in the world our children will inherit. Now is the time to look at yourself, shed some of the ways you have looked at and handled money and set a new way forward for your kids. You not only don't have to keep carrying this baggage around, but you also don't have to pass it on to your kids. By the way, Grandma and Grandpa should also discuss the worksheet, take this quiz, and share the results with your kids, so that together you can set new goals for your grandchildren.

This next worksheet will help you create a paradigm, a template of your household's financial personality. I've even thrown in some "non-financial" patterns as well, that could have a monetary value, if you were to subcontract out those responsibilities. None of this is meant to be judgmental—there's no single right or wrong way to run a household. The questions are designed to help you find out where you are now and how that jibes with the financial paradigm, you'd ideally like to see for your kids. You will note that I have separated "Goal Setting" from "How It Works Out." Does that actual handling of your finances match your goal of how you want to handle your money life? Here is a chance to reflect upon that and to discuss it openly with your partner.

Earning:

Goal Setting

Who makes decisions as to who works, who stays home?

What is the basis of the decision?

- One person to stay home with the kids?
- One person to go to school?
- Traditional male breadwinner attitude?
- Necessity of two incomes?
- No choice-single-parent family?
- Elderly parents to consider?
- Other?
- Whose job takes priority if a move is necessary or desirable?

How It Works

Who earns the money in your family?

- Male partner(s)
- Female partner(s)
- Two-income family
- Single parent

Are there other sources of income?

- Inheritance
- Current gifts from in-laws, parents, and the like
- Investments

Saving:

Goal Setting

Who makes the decisions on goals for which the family is saving/investing?

Who makes the investment vehicle decisions?

How much is the decision-making process shared or explained to the non-involved party?

Who makes the decisions on the family's insurance goals and strategies?

Who makes the insurance plan decisions? Who owns the policies?

How It Works

Who does the day-to-day, month-to-month work of saving/investing?

Who handles the bank accounts?

Who has access to all funds?

Who has keys to the safe-deposit box?

Who has contacts with the following?

- Financial planners/investment professionals
- Online investments/banks
- Bank/finance company holding your mortgage/car loan or lease
- Insurance agents
- Accountants
- Lawyers

Spending:

Goal Setting

Who makes small-item buying decisions?

How much and what kind of input from other family members?

Who makes large-item buying decisions?

How much and what kind of input from other family members?

Who makes medical expenditure decisions?

How It Works

Who does the small item buying?

Who does the large item buying?

Who's in charge of the weekly household budget?

Who picks out and purchases gifts?

Do you have joint or separate accounts?

Do you have a household account where you co-mingle some funds?

Is your home owned jointly? How does the title read? How does the mortgage read?

Who has the title to your car(s)?

Who sets up medical appointments and pays those bills?

Sharing Within The Household:

Goal Setting

Who sets out the goals around running the household and caring for the kids?

How It Works

How are household responsibilities divided?

- Kitchen chores?
- Cleaning chores?
- Repairing chores?
- Child care chores (including finding daycare and sitters)?
- Who takes kids back and forth to daycare/ school/doctors?
- Who goes to games and plays and other activities?
- Who stays home if the kids are sick?
- Who helps with homework?
- Yardwork?
- Dog walking?
- Pet care?
- Other?

Sharing in the Larger Community:

Goal Setting

Who sets goals as to charitable giving?

How It Works

Who makes decisions about charitable giving?

What charities? How much?

Who makes decisions about giving time/volunteering to socially conscious activities?

What activity? How much?

Which of these patterns do you want to pass on to your children? Which ones do you hope they'll avoid?

Let It Go

Think about this: If you've fallen into patterns that are not what you'd want your children to be learning, maybe they aren't the best ones for you to be in, either. One of the best times to take stock of ourselves is precisely at this time: when we're thinking about what we want for our children.

On the other hand, some of the patterns in your life may work for you while others may not fit into the brave new world that our kids face today. For many households of baby boomers, the mom-staying-at-home-with-the-kids' paradigm worked very well indeed. Our parents and our parents' parents may certainly have embraced that paradigm. It's no criticism of Grandma or Great Grandma to say that it's no longer the only paradigm for a contemporary mother (or father). In fact, it's not even the principal one. Today, 70 percent of women[14] with children work outside of the home. Also, many Mompreneurs run at-home businesses that don't get reflected in this data. Two income families are more and more the norm. Also, lots of fathers, partnered or not, are stay-at-home dads, as well.

Understand your patterns and talk to your kids about whether or not they're expected to follow them.

WHAT KIND OF CHILD
DO YOU WANT?

Remember my Oprah families? What I suspect they meant (and as they came to understand) was that they wanted their kids to have the happiness, self-confidence, and stability that had been missing from their own childhoods. It was never about "stuff." But the stories we were taught about money help us to create new stories for ourselves...and these may not be the stories by which we want to live.

Many of us want our children to do better than we did. For generations of American life, we've been accustomed to measuring by material success, and we want our children to be financially stable. But that's just a small part of a larger package. What we really want—what I'm working toward in this book and all of my efforts—is to raise children who are happy, healthy, self-sufficient, well rounded, secure, generous, and ultimately independent—able to make the right life decisions both professionally and personally. As the Dalai Lama put it, "When educating the minds of our youth, we must not forget to educate their hearts." Isn't that what it's all about?

You must remember, as I've said, that our kids are watching us. We need to think about our money patterns early on. I think "early-on" is the second we find out we are pregnant and are going to be responsible for that little child who we will raise to be a grown adult. Okay, in utero they can't see us, but how many of us have listened to classical music, or in my case, *The Beatles*, so our unborn kids could hear great music? We start our patterns early-on. We can also change them early-on. Maybe rather than letting one of your friends or family plan that baby shower where people will give you tons of scratchy baby outfits that need to be dry cleaned, they help you to give your child a financial future. Friends will be thrilled to do that. I advise a company called EarlyBird. They offer loved ones a way to help parents save for their kids future by providing an easy-to-contribute, custodial 529 college savings program as well as other investment vehicles. This then becomes a habit that can be kept up when your child celebrates a birthday and or holiday.

SECTION II

MONEY BASICS FOR YOUNG CHILDREN: AGES 3-12

SHMOOTZ

FUN FACTS ABOUT MONEY

Kids love trivia; actually, we love trivia, too. Fun facts are a great way to get your kids interested in money. It's also a great way to make you the cool parent or grandparent!

Here are some fun facts:

- Our "paper money" is not made of paper at all. It's cloth. It's 75% cotton. In fact, in Ben Franklin's day, people repaired torn bills with a needle and thread.
- The ink used to print our money never dries. If you rub the gray side of our bills, some ink will come off. The new bills are printed with high tech ink. It is trackable, magnetic, and even can change colors. We spend all this money on this super ink because it makes it harder for people to counterfeit our bills. The bills are printed in the Bureau of Engraving and Printing in Washington, D.C.
- Which bill is counterfeited the most? The $20 bill.
- Worn out bills are composted. In fact, a farm in Delaware mulches more than four tons of U.S. cash into compost every day.
- Pennies today are made of copper and zinc. If your child buries them in a garden, they will repel slugs because they get an electric shock from touching those metals.
- It costs more than a penny to make a penny. It costs about 1.7 cents to make each penny.
- $2.00 bills are cool. They are not as rare as they seem. Over one billion of them are in circulation. You can ask your local bank to get some for your kids.

- You know when you go through airport security and your loose change dumps out of your pockets? Well, you are not alone. In 2015, the TSA reported over $750,000 in loose change at airport security checkpoints in the U.S. Who gets to keep all of that change? The TSA.
- More Monopoly money is printed each year than real money.
- What is the only rule to get your picture on our money? You have to be dead. That's because our Founding Fathers didn't want to be like the kings and queens in Europe, who have their faces on money. They didn't want anyone to have that much power.

YOUR FINANCIAL PERSONALITY

History, literature, and the media are full of references to the greedy and the generous, so much so that we call up examples of both traits just by mentioning names. Say "Scrooge" or "Jack Benny" and Baby Boomers will automatically think tightwad. King Midas loved gold so much that he made a fatal wish that everything he touched would turn to gold. If you say, "Bill Gates" or "Warren Buffett" or "Mark Zuckerberg" and are discussing charity, everyone knows that all three are funding massive foundations with their fortunes. Even historical capitalists like Carnegie, Rockefeller, and Vanderbilt are also known for a great concert hall, philanthropic foundations, and universities.

Most of us don't fall into either extreme. We don't hide in the dark to avoid giving away a few dollars worth of candy on Halloween, but we like to think we're not pushovers for every sob story that comes along either. We may not have the money to build a great university, but we can give something to our alumni fund. We may not be able to see our names on a hospital or a concert hall, but we can give to charities that mean something to us.

We all have our unique relationship to money; in general, we are either a spender or a saver. Whichever you are, that attitude toward money is going to influence how you raise your children to think about money. They watch everything we do. James Baldwin said, "Children have never been very good at listening to their elders, but they have never failed to imitate them." It's time to take stock of yourself to see if you are sending the messages you want. Those messages will be based mainly upon your view of money. Do you know whether you (and your partner) are a spender or a saver? Take this quiz to see.

YOUR FINANCIAL PERSONALITY TYPE	YES	NO
1. Do you find yourself worrying about money often?	YES	NO
2. Do you use your credit cards to the limit?	YES	NO
3. Do you know exactly how much you have saved/invested?	YES	NO
4. Do you live paycheck to paycheck?	YES	NO
5. If you suddenly received a large sum of money, would you save/invest most of it?	YES	NO
6. Do you feel that you have to prove you can live as well as people around you?	YES	NO
7. Are you afraid that you'll be left destitute in your old age?	YES	NO
8. Do you make on-the-spot decisions to buy something you like?	YES	NO
9. When your significant other suggests buying something is your first response, "We can't afford it."	YES	NO
10. Do you use shopping as a reward for yourself?	YES	NO

How To Score:

"Yes" answers to the odd-numbered questions indicate a **Saver**, while "Yes" answers to the even-numbered questions show a **Spender**. Where were most of your "Yes" answers? How do you stack up to your partners' answers?

Now it's time to decide how each of your kids and grandkids stack up with how they handle money. You are answering the questions, not your children, because you know the answers. If you have more than one child, you may find that each child has a different financial personality. Isn't it odd to think that two children raised in the same household could handle money differently? I find this so interesting. I've even worked with twins, and I have yet to find any that handle money the same way. Here goes:

WHAT IS YOUR CHILD'S FINANCIAL PERSONALITY?	YES	NO
1. If you give your child money, do they save it?	YES	NO
2. Does your child lose or misplace money often?	YES	NO
3. Is your child reluctant to spend any of their own money?	YES	NO
4. When you're shopping with your child, are the words, "I want, I want!" a familiar refrain?	YES	NO
5. Is your child proud of watching the figures in their bank account grow?	YES	NO
6. If you ask your young one, "Why do you want this?" are you likely to hear, "Because one of my friends has it," or "I saw it on TV or online"?	YES	NO
7. Does your child sometimes save up for a special toy, and then decide they don't want it that much?	YES	NO
8. If you say you are not to stopping off for ice cream or a pizza, will your child ask, "Can we if I pay for it?"	YES	NO
9. When you go out on a shopping trip, will your child always come back with some money in their pocket?	YES	NO
10. When you travel, does your youngster want to bring back presents for all of their friends?	YES	NO

How To Score:

Same as before.

And what does it all mean? First of all, it's just a quiz. It doesn't mean that you need to start worrying that you've got a miser on your hands, or the last of the big-time spenders, even if your child did score five out of five on one side or the other. These are just predispositions and can be tempered over time with common sense and education.

It does mean that if you're a saver, you're naturally going to want to teach your kids the importance of saving. If your child is a saver, you'll want to modify those lessons; rein in your natural impulses and remind both of you that money is only as good as how much happiness it allows into the world. If you're a spender and your child is a spender, get a handle on your impulses and remember that spending isn't everything. Spending will not necessarily make you or your child happy for the long run. If you're one personality and your child is the other, do not get upset that your young one isn't following in your footsteps.

The ideal financial personality is right in the middle: a careful but joyful spender, *and* a disciplined saver. That is the balance that I will be concentrating on in this book. You will never need extreme discipline to change your youngster's behavior; you need to help them set specific short-range and long-range goals for their money. The excitement of setting up a strategy to pursue these goals, and the satisfaction of attaining them, will begin to instill in your child the pure joy of money saved, and money spent. The system's beauty is that your children will see the consequences of their behavior around money spent and money saved. They will learn to own their particular behavior.

Your Rules Should Encompass Your Values:
Stick To Them

What is the most important concept to teach children about money? Most of us would say "saving money," because to many Americans it seems so hard to do. And we wouldn't be wrong; we'd only be half right. Most of our money, even for the best savers, is allocated for spending. We pay for taxes, food, medical expenses, shelter, retirement, and education. We also enjoy "discretionary spending," even though many of us can phrase it as "indiscretionary spending." Teaching children to save money is very important; showing children how to spend money wisely is equally important but involving them is most important. As Ben Franklin said, "Tell me and I forget. Teach me and I remember. Involve me and I learn."

We'd be right if we started with the lessons of saving, since the practice of not saving has created challenges for many Americans. The Federal Reserve included disturbing savings information in their *Report on the Economic Well-Being of U.S. Households in 2015.*[15] The report indicated that almost half of Americans have seriously not saved enough. "Forty-six percent of adults say that they either could not cover an emergency expense costing $400 or would cover it by selling something or borrowing money." The overall savings rate in our country is hovering around 5.5%, which is not enough for most families to plan an adequate future for themselves and their loved ones. And remember, this is an average number, so the big savers are skewing the numbers higher for the low savers. It's confusing to look at savings rates in our current situation. Many people are comfort-spending, others are hoarding money because stores and malls have been closed, and many have just plan run out of money.

TEACHING KIDS ABOUT MONEY IN THE DIGITAL WORLD

Magic card or not, it's the tangibility of money that makes it such a useful tool in teaching children how the world is structured. It is tough to do this in the world of electronics. Today, the world is digitized as more and more of us use devices and cards; even Bitcoin pays for items and bills or allows the transfer of money. When they grow up, our grand-children may think that physical bills and coins are only to be collected, like old vinyls. Soon, eye or facial recognition could allow for purchases and payments and change the whole face of banking (no pun intended). So, how do you teach children about money in this digital age?

Because this young generation of kids has grown up in the digital world, they are incredibly comfortable with the virtual universe. For me, the virtual world, when it comes to money, can become the real world almost seamlessly. If you want to see the hazards of confusing the virtual world of gameplay with the real world of money, look at the online gambling activity among young people.

To make the lessons real, I feel it is critical to start with real money, and then introduce your young ones to the digital world of money. Coins and bills are tangible and visible: kids still see it every day, they do see it being used, and they quickly grasp the general concept of how it's used. (As a matter of fact, Rhett was right, and I was wrong in that toy store – I did have money in the form of my little plastic card. I did explain how the card worked and that it didn't mean that I got things for free or by magic; it was a promise to pay the money I owed for the toy at the end of the month.) (*No, I didn't buy the toy for him.*)

Money is one of the first experiences a child has with abstract, symbolic concepts. Language is the first, and that may well be the hardest intellectual challenge a human being faces—understanding that these strange sounds big people make represent things, actions, and even feelings you can't see like hunger or sleepiness, happiness, or sadness.

If a child can work that one out, they can work out that silver coins and green pieces of paper—if they're the right ones—can be exchanged for things they really want, like toys. The question is; when do they understand this? If you ask your children what Mommy or Daddy or Grandma or Grandpa do with money, and they can answer, "They go into the store and buy things with it," then they have grasped the basic concept of using money as a *medium of exchange*. They are now ready to start these lessons. By the way, even though our kids and grandkids are going to live in a digital world, I think that real money gives them a chance to understand that the electronic money represents tangible currency. If you only start with the electronic concept of currency, you run the risk of having your little ones feel that it is only a game.

How To Explain Bitcoin To Your Grandchildren

I write for Kiplinger's, and I'm lucky enough to have Lisa Kiplinger as my editor. She and I were talking one day, and I told her I was taking a 16-hour graduate-level course on Bitcoin at Columbia Graduate School of Business. She asked why, and I said my goal was to explain it to my grandchildren. She said, "Great, that is an article."

Here is the article (or most of it):

A monetary blast from the past: To understand today's new cryptocurrencies, it helps to take a look at how currencies evolved in the first place:

Kids love stories and make-believe, so why not share the story of bitcoin with your grandkids? I realize that the tale of bitcoin and other cryptocurrencies is not fantasy, but it sure does feel that way because these new electronic mediums of exchange have been created out of "thin air."

The point is that we are in a new digital world and it is here to stay. So, as grandparents, we need to stop fighting the changes and get ahead of the curve. Who better than you to teach your grandchildren about this new world of money?

The Good Old Days Are Just That

We have seen big changes, and we adapted to them. Remember when we were so excited to be the first family on the block to get the new rotary Princess phone in sky blue or the excitement of the first mobile phone that was about the size of a shoe box and hardly worked anywhere?

Let's face it, our grandkids never knew those days and can now place and receive calls from their watches! And yes, you remember when the home video camera was invented. It was usually Dad who carried it around with that huge light bar attached. Today's youth can record video from their phones and even send those recordings out to the world with one click. I wish I could tell my grandfather, Grandpa Bill about that!

Share your stories of how it used to be with your grandkids. They need to know them. (My kids loved the stories of black-and-white television with only three channels.) These may be entertaining anecdotes, but they are also a great segue to be a vital part of their learning today. And, digital media affects every aspect of our lives, especially our interaction with money.

The new world has produced a new way to look at the old world of money. The story of money is about make-believe, because the value we give to money is not real or tangible. We give it value every time we use it to pay for something. I'm jumping ahead, but you get the point. Start the money conversation with your grandchildren with a simple explanation of why we even have money.

Why Money Was Invented

Once upon a time, about 10,000 years ago, people had to live where they could find food. Groups of people moved, from place to place, in search of something to eat. Sometimes one group of people would meet another group and see new things — new things they wanted. Then, the groups decided to trade with each other.

Trading, or bartering, was easy as long as there were only a few things to swap. Villages grew, and when there were hundreds of items to swap, the bartering system got very complicated. People had to carry around everything they wanted to trade with — and that got very difficult. In addition, it was not easy figuring out and agreeing on the value of things. You can only tell the value by knowing what people are willing to give you in exchange for it. When people bartered, they needed to agree on the value of their possessions, otherwise, no deal.

They needed an easier way to trade.

Instead of bartering or trading with each other, people sometimes used a medium of exchange. The medium of exchange
was a standard measure of value. For instance, if shells were
used as a common medium of exchange, the value of everything was measured in shells. Let's say a hat cost five shells,
and a bunch of bananas cost seven shells. People brought
their goods to market, picked out what they wanted, and
agreed upon a medium of exchange. Buying and selling
became easier.

Different items were used as a medium of exchange.

Some of my favorites are:

> Salt
> Tea leaves
> Feathers
> Seeds
> Camels
> Shells
> Dried fish
> Elephant tail bristles
> Dead rats!

But many of these mediums of exchange didn't work well.
Feathers blew away. Shells crushed. Dried fish smelled. Also,
in the case of shells, if you lived by the shore, you could collect
shells each day and be richer than the mountain people, who
had no shells.

People discovered that they needed to control the supply of
the medium of exchange to make it work. Precious metals, like
gold and silver, were hard to find. As such, they became great
mediums of exchange. Also, in those early days, kings and
queens could control the production of precious metals, and
the value could be stamped on coins to let everyone know its
worth. That is how our first coins came into being.

If you were rich, it was hard to carry all of your coins around. You left your precious metal at the goldsmith shop or jewelry store in town. These establishments had a vault, and a depositor would be given a paper receipt for the gold or silver held by the goldsmith. Goldsmiths became the first bankers, and those paper receipts became paper money. However, the Chinese are credited with printing the first easy-to-carry bills.

As time went on, there were people who didn't trust that their money was valuable, so governments, including our own, backed up their money with real gold held in vaults. As our country became economically stronger and stronger, the United States Treasury Department decided that it would be better not to have our money backed by real gold and silver. They said that our money was backed by "the full faith and credit of the United States." The concept can be hard to understand because, if everyone got scared all at once and wanted their money from banks all at the same time, we would not have enough printed money. Another fairy tale, I suppose for another time.

The Not So New World

I spoke to an expert in the cryptocurrency world, who eased my misgivings around this emerging sector. Michael Collins, Co-Founder/CEO of GN Compass, explained that, "We live in a world where we work digitally, shop digitally, buy music digitally, perform searches digitally, socialize digitally, even date digitally. So, it makes sense that we will have our money created digitally, as well. It is just the next evolution of the 400+-year-old financial system."

Collins went on to explain that, "The concept of cryptocurrency has been around since the early '90s, where different cryptographers created and developed the idea for a digital currency that was not controlled by a central bank. After the 2008 global financial meltdown, people became disenchanted with big banks and started to take a look at digital currencies as a way to store value and as a form of payment. Bitcoin was the popular platform to go live in January 2009. Since then, many others have followed suit."

What Is Bitcoin?

Now for the fun part. Remind your grandkids that a medium of exchange is anything that people agree upon to buy and sell goods or services. Also, explain to them that now, when you use a credit card or PayPal, you are using digital cash. You are not paying your bills by running around with a pile of bills and coins.

Well, a few years ago, bitcoin became a medium of exchange; a currency for people to buy and sell things. It was created and used electronically, only on the Internet. It isn't controlled by anyone. It almost seems like magic; bitcoin is a currency that was created out of thin air. And, everyone can see all of their transactions on a public ledger that people call a blockchain.

One big difference with bitcoins and our traditional currency is that when you want to send money to another person, it doesn't go from your bank to theirs: It goes directly to the person. Also, remember when I mentioned that people decided the value of something in the marketplace long ago? Bitcoins work the same way. Their value, and therefore their buying strength, goes up and down. Its value is gauged against dollars, for instance. If you have actual money, you can use some of that money to buy some bitcoins. So, let's say, perhaps you could buy a bitcoin for a dollar and maybe if lots of people think it's cool to use them demand will go up. As demand goes up, so does the price and value of the bitcoin. In fact, that's exactly what happened. It was nuts. Bitcoin hit an all-time high17 of almost $20,000 per unit in 2017!

Every time a transaction takes place, someone has to verify that it is real because it's important for everyone to trust bitcoins and to make sure that the transaction was completed only once. I think of this verification as a math game. Individuals, or a group of people, use their computing smarts on powerful computers to solve a complex math problem and come up with an answer called a nonce. They have to follow special rules. Once this problem or nonce (mathematical number) is solved, the transactions go through, bitcoins are transferred to the people or companies, and more transactions can be verified, and the next group of transactions (block) can be recorded and verified.

The person, or group of people, who work hard to solve the nonce are paid a transaction fee for their work by the bitcoin sender. They also receive bitcoins through a process called mining (a term associated with mining for gold). When they solve the nonce, they get the bitcoins. Also, just like you have a wallet for your bills and coins, bitcoin provides a digital wallet. With bitcoin you have your own secret password or private key that only you know, as well as an address key where bitcoins are sent to you. Think of it kind of like an email address for receiving emails and your private key as your email password to access and send emails. You use a person's address key to send them bitcoin, and you give someone your address key to receive bitcoins. Your private key (like a password) gives you access to your wallet and to send bitcoins. Your private key should be kept in a safe place. If you lose it, all your bitcoins are gone.

The Moral of The Story

Grandparents, you have kept up with change and, in so many cases, you were the catalyst for change. Keep embracing change and the wonderful place you hold in your grandchild's life as a purveyor of wisdom. And, remember the words of Confucius, "Life is really simple, but we insist on making it complicated."

THE ALLOWANCE SYSTEM

Work-for-Pay

Work-For-Pay may raise a few eyebrows, but I think that young children should go on the family payroll. I feel strongly that they should be getting an allowance in the form of payment for work for specific jobs---when they reach the age of three to five. Why do I start so young? Research shows that the greatest amount of brain growth occurs between birth and age five.[18] In fact, by age 3, roughly 85% of the brain's core structure is formed, and the cognitive processes develop in the first few years of life. So, if our children are learning the most at this young age and creating their patterns and habits, why wouldn't we start teaching them about this important life skill when they are young?

I appreciate that not all parents feel that their young ones are prepared for this, so let me say a bit about the philosophy before I get down to details. Kids are born with a sense of entitlement, which they need as infants. And they *are* entitled, as infants, to have all their needs met. I'm certainly not trying to say that will change drastically by the time your child reaches the age of three, or even five. But it will change before you know it, and I absolutely believe --- and I've seen this prove out, time after time – that even three is not too young to begin teaching life's valuable lessons. Our young ones begin at even a younger age to learn the most difficult of all tasks. As discussed above, they learn language, which is based upon complex abstractions. Their brains are ready for these lessons, which ultimately shape their habits and patterns in the real world from a young age.

One of life's other important lessons is this: The natural consequence of life is that money follows work. Remember "Get It/Spend It/Save It/Share It"? "Get It" has to come first. There are basically only two ways to get money—someone gives it to you out of the goodness of their heart, or you earn it. In the ordinary course of life, no one is going to provide you with enough to enable you to get by, and you probably wouldn't feel that good about yourself if you did live like that.

The more you go on just giving money to your kids and grandkids, the more you are fostering entitlement. Don't be surprised if they learn that lesson and keep expecting what you have taught them to expect. Robert Fulghum brought the point home when he said, "Don't worry that children never listen to you; worry that they are always watching you."

But will they understand the life consequences part? Look at it this way. Kids can learn lots of life lessons when they are three to five years old – brushing their teeth, avoiding strangers, and stopping at red lights. Do kids understand why they have to do it— or, at first, *that* they have to do it? Maybe not—they have to be reminded of each one of these rules a million times. They may not understand the principles behind long-term dental hygiene, for example, however, they brush their teeth when you show them how (and if you keep telling them). Gradually, they absorb the lesson and the reasons behind it, and, in many cases, these lessons become habits for a lifetime.

We tend to feel differently about money. It's one thing to tell your three-year-old to brush their teeth—but isn't it much too early to burden them with the concept of financial responsibilities and obligations? Well, maybe it is. But just because your child isn't ready to understand the concept of traffic control, or precisely what a speeding car can do to them, would you hold off teaching them to stop at a red light?

Your young one *is* prepared to understand what money does and is ready to start earning it. How do you structure your child's earning of the money, and—equally, if not more important—how do you structure their spending, saving, and sharing?

How Do You Explain An Allowance To A Young Child?

Make allowance simple and get them excited about the new "grown-up" program that you are going to start. Relish in the fact that your young children think you are smart and want to do things with you... and here's a concept; they want to please you and make you proud of them.

Begin with a child's definition of an allowance: *Money that a child earns each week by working within the home.* Explain that parents and grandparents make money by working at their jobs.

Citizen-of-the-Household

Work-For-Pay is an allowance based on a specified series of chores *over and above* what is expected, either as part of either their personal development or in their typical role as a contributing member of your household.

A child, in my opinion, should never be paid for:

- ✓ brushing their teeth;
- ✓ going to the potty;
- ✓ going to bed on time; or
- ✓ crossing at the green light

Kids shouldn't earn an allowance for any act relating to personal hygiene or the development of personal responsibility and self-discipline.

Your kids should also not be paid for what I call "Citizen-of-the-Household Chores." These will vary from family to family, but the general rule is this: Citizen-of-the-Household Chores are whatever everyone in the household is generally expected to chip in and do. Good citizens chip in and help. Later these lessons will become life lessons when they need to learn to be good citizens of the community, and eventually, good citizens of the world. A good citizen of the community voluntarily picks up litter and throws it away, without looking for payment. A good citizen of the world recycles and saves resources because they want the world to be a better place for everyone. The lessons have to start small, so your home is the perfect training ground.

You get to set the rules. In my household, Citizen-of-the-Household chores included:

- ✓ Returning toys to the toy box
- ✓ Putting clothes in the hamper
- ✓ Hanging up wet towels

Work-for-pay chores are whatever you designate as a "special" chore that will become the child's responsibility (for that week, anyway; tasks can be changed or rotated between children if you have more than one). Work-for-pay chores for a three to six-year-old could include the following:

- ✓ Dusting
- ✓ Sorting recyclables
- ✓ Setting the table

Note: The jobs for young children are all "helping" jobs; they are *not* taking on full responsibility for a job that they are not ready to handle. You would not ask a young child to dust a whole room, but you could show them how to dust a table; then, supervise their work.

Citizen-of-the-Household Responsibilities

As discussed, the reward for work is pay, the reward for good behavior (being a good citizen) is behavioral. Later in life, we help each other willingly and can't measure the good feelings, but for a child, we want to celebrate and reinforce good behavior for a child. When I say "celebrate," I mean by acknowledging their good behavior and fulfilling their responsibilities to themselves and the family. Praise is a reward in and of itself.

In fact, we know that praise really counts for people. Many employees would rather receive praise than a bonus. People want to feel that they are contributing to their workplace and are valued. We are social beings, and that praise gives us a sense of belonging.

I believe that, basically, children learn values at home. If your child has a consistent pattern of appropriate behavior, and they see family rules and standards at work, they will be getting the best possible lessons in proper behavior. The Citizen-of-the-Household chart is an excellent tool in reinforcing these habits. As your preschooler gets older and takes on more responsibilities, the chart will not be needed; you will just develop this into a system of rewards and punishments. For the little ones, you are trying to establish a win-win situation. You want to stress the idea that "this is what we do," much more than "this is what will happen to you if you don't."

Here are some things you are going to consider putting on each child's Citizen-of-the-Household chart. On that chart, put the list of each of the responsibilities each child will have. Most of these activities will be done each day. Just as with their Work-For-Pay chores, you model the behavior, they do the task with you until they can do it by themselves. They check off when they have finished the task, and you put a sticker or a gold star next to each completed item. You will make up your own list, but here is a sample:

Responsibilities for Children Ages 3-6

- ✓ Brush teeth (morning)
- ✓ Brush teeth (evening)
- ✓ Pick up toys
- ✓ Go to bed when you are told
- ✓ Get up when you are told
- ✓ Make your bed
- ✓ Put clothes in the hamper
- ✓ Hang up wet towels

Responsibilities for Children 7- 12

You will delineate the Citizen-of-the-Household responsibilities for your older kids. Most of these will have to do with curfews, personal hygiene, cleaning up the things left in public spaces, and helping out when you ask for help. In other words, if you are struggling with the grocery bags and ask for help, you expect them to pitch in instead of saying, "What will you pay me?" Again, you hopefully will not need a chart.

Start The Conversation With Your Kids

You may get some push back from your older kids around Citizen-of-the-Household chores. You are trying to impart your values around this critical concept. Like countries, households run on the idea of citizenship. We all share a planet, a country, a community...and a family. Good citizens try to do their part to make all of these institutions better for everyone. The following list is a funny "Conversation-Starter" and may get the point across and make your kids smile at the same time.

Read these to your child and let them respond.

WHOSE JOB IS IT?

1. **If you spill something in your bedroom, who cleans it up?**
   a. You
   b. Mom or Dad
   c. Grandma
   d. The dog (well, sometimes, if you're lucky)

2. **After you use a dish, you should:**
   a. Rinse it and put it in the dishwasher
   b. Leave it for Mom or Dad
   c. Break it—who needs used dishes?
   d. Leave it for the dog (well, maybe, but you still have to put it in the dishwasher)

3. **What do you do with your coat when you come into the house?**
   a. Hang it up in the closet or on the coat rack
   b. Leave it for Mom, Dad or Grandma
   c. Wear it all evening, including to bed
   d. Leave it on the floor in case the dog wants to wear it

4. **After you finish playing on your computer or laptop, you should:**
   a. Turn it off
   b. Leave it on (you never know if Grandma wants to play Grand Theft Auto)
   c. Turn it facing the wall
   d. Leave it for the dog—he's a big fan of "TikTok"

5. **If you turn on a light when you enter a room...**
   a. Turn it off when you leave
   b. Leave it on for Mom or Dad – who knows, maybe they are afraid of the dark
   c. Leave it on because no one showed you how to turn it off
   d. The dog will turn it off later; you taught him how

Your Young Child's Citizen-Of-The-Household Chart

How Work-For-Pay Allowance Works

You decide when your child is ready. They will start doing new chores around the house, and they will be getting paid for working. The money will belong to them. Earning your own money is very empowering. It's hard to earn money and they will pause before spending it. Thomas Jefferson quipped, "Never spend your money before you have earned it."

Start explaining this to your child well in advance of their birthday, so it becomes an exciting rite of passage to becoming a big kid.

You should not have any trouble introducing this system— young ones like to be helpful and feel grown-up. And you are laying necessary groundwork here — teaching the concept of money as part of a continuum. "Getting" money doesn't exist in isolation from earning money.

Chores for Children Ages 3 - 6

Note: Remember, you are doing the chores with your kids and modeling the behavior for them. If they can start doing the tasks on their own, let them. Rotate the chores each week.

- ✓ Bring napkins to the table
- ✓ Bring silverware (except knives) to the table
- ✓ Take napkins from the table – put in recycling or garbage
- ✓ Dust one area of a room
- ✓ Vacuum a couch or chair
- ✓ Put papers into the recycling bin
- ✓ Water plants

CITIZEN of the HOUSEHOLD chart

Opportunity

Penny
Bright

Name _____ **Week of** _____

CHORE LIST

		Saturday	Sunday	Monday	Tuesday	Wednesday	Thursday	Friday
1)	Chore Complete							
	Well Done							
2)	Chore Complete							
	Well Done							
3)	Chore Complete							
	Well Done							
4)	Chore Complete							
	Well Done							
5)	Chore Complete							
	Well Done							

✓ Feed animals
✓ Carry small trash cans (bedroom) to a larger pail

Chores for Children 7 - Teenage Years

You will model the proper way to do chores, even for your older children. Then, they are on their own. Their system works the same, but there is a significant difference. "No work, No pay." The "no work, no pay" concept includes nagging them three times during the week. And, while they still have to do their work, they won't get paid. Ouch! Remember, you are teaching them to be ready for the real world. Wouldn't you get fired if your boss always reminded you of unfinished tasks?

Feel free to adjust the number and frequency of chores for the older ones. Here's a good starting point:

--Four small chores five times a week and two large chores once a week. Work with your older kids to complete tasks around school assignments, sports, and other responsibilities. My suggestion is that as soon as they get home from school, that they can eke out 15 minutes to perform these chores — before they start texting their friends to say how unfair and lame this is!

Again, they say when the chore is completed, and you inspect the task. You will know when it's time to scrap the chart, but I would always make it clear as to what jobs they have for the week.

✓ Set the table
✓ Clear table-put dishes in the dishwasher
✓ Scrub pots and pans
✓ Collect clothes from hampers and bring to the laundry room
✓ Separate whites and colors
✓ Sweep a room

✓ Dust
✓ Vacuum
✓ Tie up recycling
✓ Be in charge of composting
✓ Take garbage to the bin
✓ Bring in mail
✓ Feed animals
✓ Weed

The Job Chart: Ages 3-6

Make up a list of chores that your child can handle. They should do about three tasks four times a week. Don't make this a burden; you can be the judge. It should not take you and your child any longer than 15 minutes to complete the tasks.

Make a job chart for each child and make sure that there is plenty of room for a big checkmark or a gold star to show completion of the chore. Put it in a prominent place, like on the refrigerator. You will show your young one how to do this, because they may not read yet.

Explain all the chores on the chart and how they will be doing them. You will let them make a big checkmark when they have completed the task, and you will "inspect" to make sure that they did a great job. A gold star sticker is always a good visual reward.

Note: If your children are older, skip the clever sticker. The principle is the same, however. They have a list of jobs that need to be completed and inspected before paying the money.

How Much Do They Earn?

I strongly recommend—in fact, this is one of the keys to making the whole program work—that you pay them enough money that they can really set goals and budget,

Work-For-Pay Chart

Small Change

Shmootz™

Name _____ **Week of** _____

CHORE LIST		Saturday	Sunday	Monday	Tuesday	Wednesday	Thursday	Friday
1)	Chore Complete							
	Chore Well Done							
2)	Chore Complete							
	Chore Well Done							
3)	Chore Complete							
	Chore Well Done							
4)	Chore Complete							
	Chore Well Done							
5)	Chore Complete							
	Chore Well Done							

but not so much that the entire process is unrealistic. This balance is hard. I think that you should pay your kids their age. So, in other words, a four-year-old would earn $4.00 per week, and a ten-year-old would receive $10.00 per week. If this does not fit into your budget, pay them half of their age per week. Stick to a schedule and make sure that the kids get a raise on each birthday.

Pay Day

"Pay day" must become part of the ritual. I like Fridays because they are a natural end of the week. Let your child review all of the boxes on their Job Chart. When all chores are complete, it's time for payday. Please make sure that you have enough coins and bills to pay your kids their hard-earned salary. Can you imagine if your employer kept handing you IOU's and said, "I'll pay you next week?" "I don't have enough money right now." Since you are going to start your young ones off with real coins and bills, you will have to stop at the bank to get enough currency. You can make one big trip every few months to make sure that you have enough on hand.

Visually count out the money and allow your child to feel that proud sense of accomplishment. Seeing the money is also a great way to teach your children coin and bill recognition. It's essential to start a Work-For-Pay system as a positive experience. So, remember that while "no pay until all the chores are done" is a good rule to implement right from the start, you also want to make sure that your child does finish all of their chores and gets the reward of money. Even though you are doing the tasks together, make sure that your kids do the actual work---they'll be so happy when you say, "You did it!!" Stay with them, make it fun, and make sure that your child finishes each chore. I know you are all very busy, but you can eke out 15 minutes for these chores when you understand that you are teaching your kids values and life skills that will last for a lifetime.

Moving Into The World Of Digital Money

As we discussed earlier, I feel that it is vital for your children to start with real tangible money.

Remember, you are only using real money until you are confident that your child can understand the concept of digital money. I am an advisor to a company called Greenlight. They offer a debit card that kids can use under supervision by parents. I like this card because parents can have real-time control for its usage, and kids get to experience some real-time spending. Greenlight lets parents choose the exact stores that make them comfortable. As soon as your kids understand this, it's time to set up their bank accounts and Greenlight debit card.

When you know that kids have a real knowledge of this process, you can begin to pay them with virtual money. I will note how to do this in each of the budget categories.

TIME FOR THE BUDGET:
THE FOUR JAR SYSTEM

Budget is a word that most adults rank right up there with a root canal and cleaning the oven as their most "favorite" responsibilities. Like sticking to a diet, almost every adult struggles from time-to-time to live within a budget.

A budget does not have to be an instrument of torture. It is merely an organizing tool designed to help one manage money more effectively. I like to consider a budget as a road map, a plan that gets you from here to your financial goal down the road. Can you imagine if you could instill this habit in your kids when they were young? Even better, can you imagine looking forward to budgeting money? You can give this gift to your kids. Tell your kids that a reasonable budget enables you to pay for what you need and save for what you want.

Get four clear plastic jars or four clear plastic envelopes and label them: *Charity; Quick Cash; Medium-Term Savings*, and *Long-Term Savings.*

Charity Jar: 10% comes off the top of your child's allowance for charity. Count out the correct amount and let your child put that in the Charity Jar or envelope.

Charitable giving is a subject close to my heart and something that I have emphasized with my children and grandchildren since they were young. It is a lesson with a high impact on a child or young adult and, again, is an opportunity for you to impart your values to your youngster. It's also a great time to get grandparents involved to share their favorite charitable giving with the grandchildren.

We give charitable donations in many ways, from offering change to a homeless person on the street (a powerful visual lesson to a child who can see that there are those less fortunate) to giving to a specific charity that you and your child pick together; to collecting PPE for local front-line workers or neighbors. We have lived through a disaster that the kids hear about online or from their friends. They want to be part of the solution, as we all do, and contribute. Or they could give to a cause, like protecting the environment or supporting a local playground. You can tithe to your local religious group that could be, in turn, helping the needy.

Remember to explain to your kids that giving is not just about giving money. Charity also means giving of yourself and your time, as well. For instance, some people volunteer their time to work in a soup kitchen or read to the blind. Many people have volunteered to deliver meals to people who couldn't get out during the pandemic. Your youngster might want to consider recycling some of their old clothes or toys that are in good condition to go to a local children's hospital. Work with them to come up with suggestions.

Digital Giving: If and when you go digital with your child, show them how you have transferred their Charity money and tell them that it is placed safely in yours (or their) checking account. When they have saved enough, you can show your child how you are transferring their charity money to the cause of their choice. Let them watch you as you go online; it will make it more real for them.

Quick Cash Jar: Divide the remaining allowance, or 90%, into thirds. The next 30% goes into this jar. Again, count out the proper amount and let your child put that in the correct jar or envelope.

Think of this as instant gratification. Your child has worked hard for their money and this allows them to spend some guilt-free on anything they impulsively want. You, of course, set the overall perimeters. If it's no chocolate or bubble gum, those are the rules. But, beyond that, let them decide. It's tough for parents to stay out of the decision-making of a young child. Remember, they are learning how to make valuable decisions. Besides, if they spend all of their Quick Cash now, they will not have anything left and have to wait until their next pay day. It's a real-life lesson. Please do not supplement this spending...and beg grandma and grandpa not to whip out that extra $20 to slip to your young ones.

Digital Quick Cash: You will again give your child a receipt for their Quick Cash; keep the allotted amount in your checking account, or transfer it to their debit card. You and your kids will have to keep track of their spending each week as you pay for what they have purchased.

Medium-Term Savings Jar: The next third or 30% goes into this jar. Again, count out the proper amount of bills and coins and let your child put them in the correct jar or envelope.

You are teaching your child to push off instant gratification and to set a savings goal to get something they want. The younger kids can only save for a few weeks because they (or you) will forget what they are saving for. Steer them toward categories that will fit within their earning power.

Take them into a store or go online and let them pick out the item they want. Suggest to your kids that they could draw a picture of the item and place it on their jar or envelope to build the excitement of earning and saving for a goal. You are teaching deferred gratification, but you are also teaching gratification—three weeks is a long time for a four-year-old.

Digital Medium-Term Savings: Again, you will give a receipt for your kids' savings and allow them to add up their money each week to see how close they are to their goal. When it comes time to spend the money, make sure that they can see the transaction on your credit or their (or your) debit card so that they start to connect their buying power with the virtual world of money. As your children get older, 12-15, I think it is really essential to set up a separate checking account with debit card privileges. In most cases, if you feel uncomfortable with your child having access to cash, you can arrange a debit card without ATM access. It's safer if kids don't have access to too much cash.

Long-Term Savings Jar: The last third, or 30%, goes into the *Long-Term Savings* jar. Again, count out the proper amount and let your child put that in the correct jar or envelope.

Long-term savings gives a child a sense of investment in their future. I know that you are thinking, "Does a four-year-old possibly understand the concept of long-term savings?" My answer would be, "Absolutely, not." "Does a ten-year-old understand the concept of long-term saving?" My answer to that is also, "Absolutely, not." Ironically, if I ask, "Do the adults in the United States understand the concept of long-term saving? My answer is, "Absolutely, not." Given that backdrop, think of long-term savings as teaching a habit that your kids need for life.

Remember how you are teaching your kids to brush their teeth as young ones, when they do not understand the concept of oral hygiene? Think of these money lessons in the same way. Tell them that they are saving for college, or whatever the long-term goal, and eventually they will understand. It's now time for a trip to the bank to set up a savings account for your child.

Digital Long-Term Savings: Open up a savings account in your child's name (see below) with you as the guardian. Show them their statement online and how they earn interest. Again, give your child a weekly receipt for their money and point out how the money is deposited into their new savings account.

Note: If you tie this account to yours, your bank may waive any fees.

But, Do The Kids Absorb All Of This?

Yes. Okay, maybe not all, but some, I promise. I had one tear-jerker moment of, "Yes...OMG, they get it," with my son Rhett when he was five years old. We were going to a local corner grocery store in Manhattan so he could spend his Quick Cash. I was liberal on allowing him Tootsie Roll Pops. I sat in the back of the store while he figured out how many Pops he could buy with his Quick Cash. He proudly held his Quick Cash in one and his Pops in the other and went into the queue. In front of him was a homeless woman who had a cup of change and one orange. She placed these on the counter, and the salesman counted out her change. He told her that the orange cost 33 cents and that she did not have enough money and gave her back her change.

My five-year-old was listening to this, and as the woman walked away, he said, "Excuse me, I would like to buy that orange for you." She looked down, and said sweetly, "No, I can't let you do that."

All eyes were on this little kid...

He said, "No, you don't understand, this is my *Quick Cash*, and I get to spend it any way I want. I want to buy you this orange. I just have to put my Tootsie Rolls down and start over counting my money."

She was still insistent that she was not going to take money from this child. He was, of course, equally emphatic.

He quipped, "Didn't you read my Mother's book? (Evidently, she hadn't.) These are the rules. I work for a living, and I want to buy you this orange, because when someday I don't have money, someone will be there to buy me an orange."

Every woman in the store burst out into tears... including me.

Rhett sat down, recounted his money, and bought the woman the orange. Then, he came back to where I was waiting.

"In between my sniffles, I choked out, "I'm so proud of you." To which Rhett said, "Didn't you read your book? These are the rules. You are supposed to be proud of me when I surprise you and do something I'm not expected to do, not when I do what I should be doing."

That was a sobering moment. Do they "get it"? Yes.

FIELD TRIP: VISITING A REAL BANK OR CREDIT UNION

These are the basic documents you will need for your child to have a guardianship bank savings or checking account tied to your account:

- ❐ Latest photograph
- ❐ Relationship document – you need to prove that they are your child (a birth certificate will prove that)
- ❐ Identity proof (birth certificate)
- ❐ Proof of address (show that their address is yours or your partners – a letter from school will work)
- ❐ Social Security Number

Hopefully, your child already has some idea of what a bank is, even if they have heard you talk about your online bill-paying account, or it may have been when they were in the car with you while you drove through the teller's drive-through window. You want this real visit to be meaningful because soon, your kids will enter into the virtual world of banking.

First, explain that a bank is a safe place to keep the money. Money in their piggy bank or allowance jars can be lost or stolen if they are carrying it around. Banks insure our money, so we never have to worry about it being there when we need it. Banks then rent our money to other people so they, in turn, can buy houses and cars, for instance. The bank pays us for the use of our money, and that little bit they pay us is called *interest*.

Explain to your kids that the bank communicates with you online. So, as soon as you know that the account is set up jointly for you and your child, show them the account online. They will start to connect the real and virtual worlds of finance.

Have your child save their long-term money in their jar for a month or two, so you are not making too many trips to the bank.

TAKING STOCK FOR
YOUNG CHILDREN

When your kids are around ten years old, it is time to introduce them to investing in the stock market. I have included a child's explanation of what stocks are and basically why companies issue them and then why you, as a shareholder, would buy stock. You can read these italic sections to your young ones.

It's In Stock

Suppose your own a business, such as a lawn-mowing service. But you don't have enough money to buy a new lawnmower you need. What could you do to get more money? You could borrow money, or you could invite friends to share in the cost of your business—for a profit of course.

The example above is similar to what companies do when they need money to expand or grow. Companies sell stock. Stocks are like bricks in a building. If you own a brick, you own a share, or part of the building. Owning a stock means that you are a stockholder or shareholder---a part owner of the company. So, you own a share of everything the company owns.

Opening Up To Shareholders

When the company's owners decide they want to sell stock in their company, they "go public." Public means that the owners sell shares to anyone who wants to buy them. How many shares do they sell? It's up to the owners of the company. It could be one hundred, one thousand, one million, or more.

Having A Say In The Company

Congratulations! You've bought stock! When you hold stock in a company, you can have a say about running the company. Every year, the company invites shareholders to an annual shareholders meeting. At the meeting, you may vote on specific future company plans. Every share is worth one vote. As you might have guessed, the more shares a person has, the more power they have in company decision-making.

It Can Be Good To Stock Up

Why do people buy stock? To make money. You want your stock to be worth more than what you paid. If the company does well, you can expect the value of your shares to go up. If you decided to sell your shares, you would receive more money than you paid. You can hold onto your shares for as long as you want. You choose when you want to sell them. You may also receive dividends, which are part of the company's profits. Some of the profits are split among stockholders, who usually receive dividends every three months or so.

Good Times and Bad

What happens if the company that you own stock in has a loss? The value of your shares would probably go down. Investing in stocks can be tricky!

As a part-owner of the company, you must take the good times with the bad. There is always a risk that your shares' value can go down so far that you lose the money you invested in the company. So, before you buy stock in a company, you should go online and do some research. What does the company do? How long has it been around? Has it been successful?

Who's Selling?

You've done your research, and you've decided to invest some money in a particular company. Where do you go? When you want to buy or sell stocks, you contact a stockbroker, or a person who buys and sells shares of stock for customers. Stockbrokers are paid a commission, or fees, on the stocks they buy and sell.

This Is Some Market!

If you ever listen to news reports on TV or radio, or see stock prices online, you might have heard about stocks rising and falling. What does that mean? The prices are going up and down. The stock market, where shares are bought and sold, determines the price of stocks. Stock prices can change almost instantly. The stock market is like a supermarket for buying and selling shares in different companies.

The price of the shares will go up if many people want to buy a share in a company. If many people want to sell shares in a company, the price will go down.

How To Start Your 10 Year Old's Investing In The Stock Market

Legally your kids have to be 18 to own stocks, so the purchase will be done in your name. You can open a custodial account. Have them find out how much they have in their Long-Term Savings Account at the bank. It's great if you could match that, if you can afford it.

Let the kids research about five companies they know, like Nike, Apple, Amazon, Walmart, Disney, etc. I want them to start by investing in companies they know. There are many mobile investing apps that you can use. If you research, there are apps that permit you to buy fractional shares. I work with a company called DriveWealth, who has a mobile investing app. I am impressed with their flexibility for the small investor, because they offer fractional shares. A fractional share means that you can buy a piece of one share. Shares can be very expensive, so this is a great feature. Even though you are doing the investing on behalf of your kids, they will be excited that "their" portfolio can include many fractional shares.

They have to present their research to you. It may turn up some interesting facts, such as "Disney owns ESPN and ABC and Marvel." So, start the conversation with your kids around their and other kids' behavior and how that could influence their stock pick. For instance, if lots of people went to see the new Marvel movie, what could happen to Disney stock (it could go up). And what would happen if gas prices went up and it was too expensive to drive to Disney World? What could happen to Disney stock? Even mention things like the pandemic. People had to social distance and couldn't go to theme parks. What do they think happened to Disney stock? Do they think that that was permanent, or temporary, as the country opened up again with new regulations regarding social distancing? Explain that there is not necessarily a direct correlation, but you just want to get them thinking.

The next step is to explain that the best strategy is to purchase shares and hold onto them when you believe in a company. If you hear bad news and see the share price dropping, you are selling at a low point. And if conversely, if there is good news and the stock price starts to go up, you are buying at a high price. Also, explain that the brokers have great computers that follow every tick of the stock market. They watch their screens all day. It's so hard to guess when a stock is going to go up or down. It's always best to invest regularly and buy and hold your shares.

Miracle of Compounding

There is another crucial concept to teach your kids, the *Miracle of Compounding*. Compounding is a superpower, especially for your young kids, because they have lots of time to invest. But the secret is to leave the money in the investment: both the original amount (principal) they invest plus the interest or gains they earn. Why? Because this magic force leads to more money over and over again.

Example:

Let's say your 10-year-old has already saved $250 in their Long-Term Saving, and it's in a bank. Now you invest that money with them in the stock market. They can take a little risk, but on average, let's say they invest for 55 years until they are 65 years old. I'll be conservative and say they only invest $100 a month, earning 10%. By the time they are 65 years old, they will have over $1.2 million. Now let's say they can invest $200 a month at the same rate. Your child will have almost $2.4 million at age 65.

Now let's say that they wait until they are out of college to start to save, and they begin the same program of $200 a month, but now can only save for 40 years. At age 65, they will only have about $700,000.

Now let's say they wait until they are 40 to save. Your child will only have about $200,000.

The greatest genius in the world, Albert Einstein, once said, "Compound interest is the most powerful force in the universe."

(Note: I encourage you and your children to check out the interest rate calculators online. Play with the numbers so that this lesson resonates with them... and you.)

ACTIVITIES FOR PARENTS AND GRANDPARENTS TO DO WITH YOUNGER CHILDREN

Show And Tell

Games encourage a tangible relationship to money for your young children and grandchildren. Some games include money identification, stacking and counting, and change-making. For all of these games, use real money, not play money. Toddlers can swallow coins, so make sure that you closely supervise them and take the money away after playing.

Money Identification Games

Below are basic games; the first ones you'll teach. You can also invent your own. Very young children won't fully understand concepts of value at first, but they can understand games of "how much." They must be able to see, and be able to identify, the physical substance of money before they can do anything with it. You want them to start becoming familiar and comfortable with the value it represents.

Coin Identification Game

Goal: To tell the difference between coins.

You'll Need: Four plastic jars or containers, each of them marked with all the names of the coin that jar will represent. The penny jar will be labeled "Penny, 1c, One Cent"; the nickels jar "Nickel, 5c, Five Cents", and so on. Put a few coins of the proper denomination in each jar to start the ball rolling. You will also need a big stack of coins of different denominations. It's not that usual to see half dollars or dollar coins anymore, so you can save those for later, when you can make the game harder.

Rules: First, pick up a coin from your pile, tell your child what it is, and have your child repeat the name of the coin and then put it in the proper jar. Do that with every coin jar. Next, you can add another challenge by naming the coin and asking your child to give the other name(s) for the coin. For example, a penny, or one cent.

What It Teaches: Recognizing different coins by appearance, identifying them by name. Since the jars are picked up and put away at the end of each game session, an ancillary lesson is one of being neat and also for having responsibility for your belongings. You are starting to teach your child that money needs to be put in a safe place.

Small-Change Game

Goal: To show a child how to count money and understand its value.

You'll Need: A pile of coins and bills. You can also conduct a treasure hunt where your young ones can gather up all of the loose change in the house. Don't forget the pockets of coats and jackets, drawers, old purses, and under the sofa cushions! You can stash some coins, just to add to the excitement. Many people have a place to collect coins in a drawer or jar, or by their bedside table.

Rules: At the kitchen table, help your little ones divide the "treasure" into piles of pennies, nickels, dimes, and so forth.

How To Win: See how many combinations of coins your child can create that add up to $1. Are there twenty nickels? Or are there ten nickels and two quarters? If your young one comes up with three or more combinations, they win!

Your child or grandchild will be impressed by the size of the pile created by one hundred pennies. Seeing the stack of pennies is an excellent moment to emphasize the value of a dollar and how hard someone must work to earn that money.

THE TWEEN - AND TEEN-PRENEUR

By the time your kids are moving into the tween and teen years, they can start moving off of the allowance system and into the real world of work. It's something that you will have to monitor very closely. When I grew up, it was safe for younger children to work outside the home; today is a different story. I do like it if your young teens, with your supervision, can start to experience the responsibility of work and an employer-employee relationship before they are thrown into the real world of work. Again, you are incubating them before they leave the nest. The teen years are also an excellent time for your budding entrepreneur to spread their wings and try out their great ideas. I am listing some ideas they could consider. Use these as conversation starters and have them discuss their talents, which could produce a side-hustle to earn extra money.

- ✓ Lawn or garden service
- ✓ Pet sitting/walking/grooming
- ✓ Snow removal
- ✓ Baby-sitting for older children
- ✓ Birthday party planning
- ✓ Coaching or lessons (tennis, baseball, roller-blading, skateboarding, or other sports)
- ✓ Computer tutor
- ✓ Help neighbors to navigate their digital devices and services
- ✓ Piano lessons
- ✓ Art lessons
- ✓ Chess lessons
- ✓ Farm stand (grow and sell veggies)
- ✓ Car wash
- ✓ Read to little kids
- ✓ Garage cleaning and then hold a sale
- ✓ Recycling service and composting
- ✓ Golf caddy
- ✓ Academic tutoring
- ✓ Pool cleaning
- ✓ Selling things on eBay for others

SECTION III

TEENS AND YOUNG ADULTS: AGES 13+

PENNY BRIGHT

THE SCARY FACTS

Why do I group teens and young adults? Because If you haven't exposed either teens or young adults to the financial facts of life, the conversations and lessons are similar. It will take more time and reinforcement to teach a teen; your young adult will breeze through the process faster. The questions you may be asking are "Is it too late to create a financially functional home when kids miraculously become teenagers or young adults? Is it possible to start with a teenager and create a financially responsible human being?" The answer is a resounding, "Yes."

Sometimes it sure seems that it may be impossible. If you have come late to the idea of developing financially responsible kids, this task can seem like trying to squeeze toothpaste back into the tube. We know teens can be challenging, and teaching them anything is very hard, especially when they think that they already know everything and that we are really stupid.

My mom used to tell me, "This won't last forever...it just seems that way." I remember when my kids were little and I used to worry about making sure that they always had a story before bed or hopefully had fun at bath time. Then they grew up into teenagers. I would have given anything to spend my time worrying about story and bath time. I'm not sure who said this, but it is so true; "The funny thing about kids is, they are the reason we lose it. And the reason we hold it together." Clearly it was a quote from a parent of teens.

But, in spite of how trying these teen years can be, lessons of financial responsibility are essential. They will follow your offspring into adulthood and is their foundation for either healthy or unhealthy relationships to money and frankly to other loved ones, as well. You are not going to preach to your offspring, you are going to mentor, and guide them and you may even learn along with them.

So, whether all of this is new to you or you've been working right along, teaching your kids money skills and values, there will be times when you'll want to throw your hands up in despair. But, of course, you can't. That is why I have written this book for you. I will be there to help you every step of the way. None of us can walk away. We're parents, or have a special child in our lives, or most importantly, we are grandparents. So, what does that mean? We keep trying; we will cling to the faith that, against all the odds, we'll get through to our kids and grandkids with the message that this is *Planet Earth*, the planet where our offspring must live.

When it comes to money issues, kids can bite back with such a vengeance, and so quickly. All of a sudden, your youth finds that they have indeed, grown up. The same way Baby Boomers found themselves staring down the short road to retirement. Where did the time go? The future becomes "now" quickly. What can happen if you don't teach your kids about money? Why is this so important to start, even if you have a teen or young adult?

I have another TV story that hit home for me. I was asked to do an intervention for a college student who was graduating with not only college loan debt, but also $19,000 in credit card debt that was building up.

I met her before the show, and we did B-roll—which is TV talk for doing some background eventually edited into the live show. I asked her what she wanted now. Her response surprised me (as I sat in her empty living room) that she had always wanted a motorcycle. (I did ask if she planned on using it as a couch...but that seemed off-topic.)

I then went over the past four years of credit card expenditures. I was astonished. About 90% of the bills were for fancy juice drinks, water, coffee, pizzas, and snacks purchased during four years at college. She hadn't paid much on her credit cards and was being charged 14% on this, and it was compounding. She was paying about $300 a month. I told her at this rate, it would take her nearly 14 years to pay this off, and during that time, she would have paid over $15,000 in interest (almost doubling the loan). It didn't sink in.

On air, unfortunately, as TV goes, we made it more visual. She wanted a motorcycle. We had two curtains: behind one, we had piled empty juice glasses, water bottles, coffee cups, and pizza boxes, and behind the other curtain, we had a $19,000 motorcycle.

As we stood behind the curtains, I said, "You could have had your motorcycle, or you could have had these drinks and pizza. You chose the drinks and pizza." It was terrible; rather than this being the big *Ah-HA* moment I wanted it to be, she burst into tears. The audience also gasped at her poor choices. My goal was never to tell her these were dumb choices; I didn't want to judge her choices. I just wanted to show her to understand her options.

(Of course, a quote by Steve Martin popped to mind, but I didn't utter a word. He once said, "I love money. I love everything about it. I bought some pretty good stuff. Got a $300 pair of socks. Got a fur sink. An electric dog polisher. A gasoline powered turtleneck sweater. And, of course, I bought some dumb stuff, too.")

The lesson here was evident. Life gets in our way, and instant gratification stares us down. We give in to the moment. We all do this. And not just with money. KFC calls to me sometimes as I drive by...and yes, every-so-often, *Extra Crispy Thighs* go home with me... (so I can put the weight on my "Extra Crispy Thighs!") But, the next day, I'm back to the kale and beet salad. Hey, I have also done this with money. I try not to use shopping as a hobby...but I have succumbed to a bauble or two. But then I go back on the budget. That's the point.

Unfortunately, this drip... drip... drip method of financial planning caught up with my TV guest. The drips turned into a puddle and then into an ocean, and she started to drown in credit card debt. And, if not checked at the door, this behavior will follow her (and us) into adulthood.

- According to the Insured Retirement Institute,[19] less than 24 percent of baby boomers are confident that they will have enough savings to last throughout their retirement years.
- Until 2007, baby boomers' average savings rate[20] was negative .05 percent. Most baby boomers have not saved nearly enough.[21] The average boomer has less than $100,000 in savings and is planning to live off Social Security benefits. Forty-five percent of boomers have zero savings for retirement.
- There is approximately $764 billion in total U.S. Credit Card debt, according to the New York Fed Consumer Credit Panel/Equifax.[22]
- As of June, 2020, 70% of U.S. adults have credit cards with 14% of people having at least 10 cards, according to the Fed.
- Average credit card debt per cardholder is, $6,200, as of February 2020, pre-pandemic, according to Experian.
- According to GoBankingRates[23] survey, 69% of Americans have less than $1,000 in savings, while 34% have no money in the bank whatsoever.

- ☠ Medical bills are the number one cause of bankruptcies in our country, according to the Kaiser Family Foundation[24] in 2019. Forty-two million people are overdue by $1,766 in medical debt, according to the Consumer Financial Protection Bureau.[25]
- ☠ Student Loan debt is not automatically discharged in bankruptcy.
- ☠ There are $1.2 trillion in total U.S. auto loan debt in 2020, according to the New York Fed Consumer Credit Panel/Equifax[26].
- ☠ On average, Americans borrow over $32,000 for new vehicles and over $20,000 for used vehicles in 2020, according to Lending Tree.[27] The average monthly payment is $550 for a new vehicle, and $452 for a leased vehicle.

Our kids are headed for the same financial train wreck that many adults are headed for, but we have a chance to change all of that. It's not okay to let them stay ignorant. Our school systems have to make sure that financial literacy lessons are mandated, and if they are not, teachers have to do their part. Financial institutions have to do their part, but first and foremost, we as parents and grandparents have to take responsibility for our teenagers' financial literacy.

Teenagers and many young adults still live under our roofs, and we're still responsible for them. They look sort of like those little kids we remember from a few years ago---but they are different.

- ☞ The amount of money involved in teenagers' lives is greater than when they were younger.
- ☞ They can earn more, spend more, and when they reach the age of maturity, get into debt more. And even without the introduction of problems, their basic maintenance levels are higher.

- The amount of trouble they can get into is worse. It can have wider repercussions, and can cost... oh, a lot more.
- Their bad habits are more deeply ingrained and harder to break.

The more time we spend working with our kids on money issues, the more we can prepare them to avoid some of these problems and deal with others. If you have been teaching your kids about financial responsibility all along, only to see the wisdom you've imparted suddenly disappear into the ozone, those early lessons haven't gone away. They are just hiding, and they'll resurface---especially if you can shift gears now and learn to deal with the special problems of teenagers or young adults and money. Our gut reaction is to always rescue our kids from challenges or from any of their mistakes. But isn't it really better to teach them how to face those challenges? Our teens, are like the flowers we plant, they will reflect the care they get.

THE GREAT NEWS – OUR TEENS AND YOUNG ADULTS WANT TO HEAR FROM US

Why do you need to talk to your Gen Z'ers (born between 1995 and 2015) about money? Because they actually listen to us. Lincoln Financial Group conducted a survey entitled; *Measuring Optimism, Outlook and Direction (M.O.O.D) of America* in 2016, and they found that 66 percent of our Gen Z generation youth actually "turn to their parents for financial advice."

Mother Teresa said it really well, and she wasn't even a parent. "You will teach them to fly your flight. You will teach them to dream, but they will not dream your dream. You will teach them to live, but they will not live your life.

Nevertheless, in every flight, in every life, in every dream, the print of the way you taught them will remain."

So, parents and grandparents, it's time to start the lessons. The Lincoln Financial Group survey also indicated that half of this generation has already opened up a savings account by age 13 (on average), which is wonderful; however, that is only putting on the training wheels for the rest of the true money management that they need to learn.

So, no matter where your teenagers or young adults are with their financial common sense, we can all work at raising our kids' consciousness to a new level of financial responsibility. That is why your role as a parent or grandparent is so important. We should begin by first looking in the mirror to see what messages we're sending to our kids. As kids grow to be teenagers, their observations of their parent's weak spots become more and more acute. They sense our uncertainties, our conflicts, and even our hypocrisies. To develop good financial habits in our kids, we have to make sure we aren't enabling their bad habits. In other words, if there is a problem in your kids' financial dynamic, there is most likely a problem in the family's financial dynamic, and everyone will need to work at changing it.

This does not—I repeat, *not* mean that it's all your fault. Placing all the responsibility on you is a barrier to solving the problem, just as much as shirking responsibility.

If your kids are irresponsible financially, they own that behavior. They have to answer for debts they have accumulated, resources wasted, and ways that they have been less-than-full citizens of the household. The first step is to recognize irresponsibility, and the next is to turn it around... these things don't just happen. Money doesn't grow on trees, and neither does financial wisdom.

I will identify negative trends that can develop with teen-agers and young adults with money---and then, I am here to help you learn how to stop them. Lack of information and misinformation are the sources of almost all negative trends in teenage behavior, and they can be hard to overcome, especially since teenagers can be devastatingly literal about information when they choose to be.

Misinformation can be the worst because kids get it from their friends, and so they tend to cling to it like gospel, with potentially spiraling negative results. Then, I'll guide you in developing positive attitudes for your teenagers and young adults and their money – and show you, your children, and grandchildren proven methods to build healthy habits that will last a lifetime. Young people need to learn the value of money, and they need to learn how to incorporate money into an overall philosophy of social, personal, and ethical values. As I've explained, money is a tool. The more we learn to understand it and use it correctly, the more it becomes a positive force in a system of values. And that understanding, more than anything, is what our teenagers need to learn from us.

The great thing about money is...it's only money. It's not love or nurturing or memories – or any of those intangibles that can't be qualified. You can count it. You can measure it. You can budget it. You can plan for it. Money is not only a tool; it's a finite tool. Being finite makes it a perfect vehicle for explaining responsibility and explaining how the world works. It is also the ideal time to tell what money can and can't do. Your children will learn what they live.

Yes, we all know that money can't buy happiness. But learning to use money responsibly can boost your self-es-teem; it can allow you to support the charities that you value; it can buy protection for your loved ones and can provide you with a stress-free future. All those things can be a large component of happiness. I like the quote by George Lorimer; "It's good to have money and the things that money can buy. But it's good, too, to check once in a while and make sure that you haven't lost the things that money can't buy."

Let's first examine ourselves and how we may be interacting with our teens and young adults when it comes to money. Take this short quiz to see if you may be sending the wrong messages about money.

Read the following questions and respond with either a YES or NO.

THE COME-CLEAN-WITH-YOURSELF QUIZ: PARENTS WITH TEENS		
If your teenager asks for money, do you fork it over? Do you give money in response to nagging?	YES	NO
Are you afraid to say, "This doesn't fit into our budget"?	YES	NO
Do you feel that your teen must have what other teens have?	YES	NO
Do you make sure that your teenage kids are out of the room when you sit down to work on the family budget?	YES	NO
Do you hide the check when you go out to a restaurant?	YES	NO
Do you use credit cards to buy stuff for your teenage kids when you know you shouldn't?	YES	NO
Have you ever spent money on your teenage kids and not let your partner know?	YES	NO
Have you ever bought something for your teens because you didn't want your ex (or other set of grandparents) to be the one(s) who got it for them?	YES	NO
Do you use a shopping trip as a reward for good behavior?	YES	NO
Do you know what your kids spend their own money on?	YES	NO

I'm a harsh grader! If you answered even one question YES, it means that you may be sending the wrong messages to your kids; ones that you don't want to be sending.

Don't be upset. I grade on a curve, and a score of one doesn't mean that you flunk out of the parent or grandparent class. We all do these things; we all probably fall into several of these categories. We're good parents and grandparents striving to be better.

Let's Take A Closer Look

Do you give in when your teenager asks for money? It's hard not to. There is simply nothing more gratifying than putting a smile on the faces of those we love most in the world, of being able to make them happy.

But this is money – it's not magic. And it's not more special or valuable than a smile on your teenager's face. Or, more significant than the hug that makes your knees go weak and leaves you walking around for the next hour. Well, until you notice that you're humming the same song that they played for you while you were yelling at them to stop changing the radio stations while you both were in the car.

And money is quantifiable – it's finite. You have a certain amount, and it has to be apportioned in a way that balances emotional well-being and the realities of dealing with a limited resource. Of course, you don't forget about the emotional well-being—not that any of us ever could or should.

Remember, in the quiz, when I asked if you were afraid to say the words, "This doesn't fit into our budget?" I didn't ask if you ever said, "We can't afford it." I learned the hard way with my then young son, Rhett, when he asked for an expensive toy, and I quickly retorted, "I can't afford it." Besides that, not meaning anything to a young child or a young adult for that matter, it probably is not the truth. If I went without eating for a week, I probably could afford the toy. Or, maybe if you didn't buy the new couch for the living room to replace the one that the dog chewed to bits, you could afford to rent the limo to take the kids to the prom. If you took out a second mortgage on the house, you could probably buy your young adult that sports car they have asked you to buy.

You see where I am going and why "I can't afford it" is not a substitute for the truth. We need to be able to say, "This doesn't fit into our budget." After you establish eye contact with your teen and say it with conviction, I promise it will get more comfortable. You'll never again fall into the trap of them guilting you into buying something that really "Doesn't fit into your budget" and that more importantly, you chose not to buy. It's hard to say and harder to disappoint them. It's alright to bring your lunch for a few months to buy the prom gown. "It's not in our budget" is an acknowledgment of that choice. More than that, it means facing up to a truth that's hard even to fathom. It's your money and your choices. The real message is; when it's their money, they get to make their choices.

THE BUDGET HIERARCHY

You not only have a right, you have a responsibility to set up a hierarchy in your budgeting. You have a right and frankly an obligation to have a different life than your kids. In some ways, that's obvious that you have different rights than your younger teens. You can drive; they can't. You can vote; they can't. You get to pay less for car insurance than your teens (especially male teens), and you can enter into legally binding contracts, get a credit card, rent a car, and get a mortgage.

In other words, all things being equal, all things *aren't* equal. Let's stop here for a moment and digest that notion because it's a truth that many of our teens may have a hard time swallowing. But think about it. Your teen may sincerely believe they *need* the latest smartphone, but if you are working in a high-tech world that demands the most sophisticated connectivity, you **need** the newest smartphone. There's a big difference between *need* and **need**.

Your kids can have input into the budget—and they should—and I'll spend more time on that later. But ultimately, it's your job. You have to be the one to say no. Remember the words, "My money, my choices." It's even hard to say. We do work for our families—we want to, we expect to. But when it comes to what happens to the bucks... the buck stops here. You are the family's CEO. You need to make decisions about allocating resources.

A considerable expense is a lesson in empowerment. You need to empower your teen to have control over their large spending decisions—both the decision making and the financing. A smartphone for a teen will fall into this category. I believe that your teen needs to be allocating some of their hard-earned money to any large purchase. If you're not allocating any of your resources—and you don't know what someone else is sacrificing for you – the sky can be the limit.

What's more, it's imperative that your children—younger children, teens, and young adults alike—understand that money is a personal possession. They know that their money is their own, and you reinforce that by respecting it. You don't take from your children; you don't "borrow" from them.

You need to reinforce this awareness when it comes to your money, too. Make sure they understand that it's not just one big communal chowder that anyone can dip into anytime they want. If you don't do that, you're giving them tacit permission to just take money from you if they decide they need money for something.

Why else are we uncomfortable with saying, "It doesn't fit into the budget"? Many of us grew up in families where money was tight, and we want to give our kids more than we had. But let's remember that we're responsible for giving our kids more than money, more than material things.

Kids need to have limits set. They need a sense of perspective, and they need to relate to money values. We teach our kids values because they'll need them to conduct their lives when they move out on their own, and the only parents or grandparents to guide them will be the ones inside them. So, we can't go on being magic mommies and grand mommies forever, pretending there are no limits. We need imposed restrictions, the product of intelligent decisions. Not "We can't afford it," but "It's not in our budget."

Start a conversation about technology and spending:

Advanced technology, constant advertising, and social media have completely transformed the commercial world over the past few decades. It's important to help kids learn to be educated consumers. Sit down with your tween and teen and go through some of these questions to see how they respond. They can also share examples of when this has happened to them. It will be fun and it also will open some valuable conversations about their spending. Again, this is a conversation starter. Your teen may explain some things to you, like; cookies hold more important things than chocolate chips!

1. The way the product looks on the internet or tv is always the way it looks when you buy it.   (T) (F)

2. If you like the celeb in the ad, it is probably a good thing to buy.   (T) (F)

3. Companies are collecting data on you online with regard to products you are buying and your buying habits.   (T) (F)

4. If something looks like a good and cheap deal with reward points or other offers, you should probably buy it.   (T) (F)

5. Social media marketing on sites is an easy way to target your buying habits which is sold to other product companies so they can advertise to you.   (T) (F)

6. If you have your own money, it is okay to buy anything you see advertised.   (T) (F)

7. Stores offering free WiFi often collect info from your social media profile or email address and they can track your activity on the web inside the store.   (T) (F)

8. If you like the video or internet show you are watching, you should like whatever they are advertising.   (T) (F)

9. Facial recognition cameras can collect data in stores that can target offers to you based upon your buying choices. (T) (F)

10. Whatever your friends have, it makes sense for you to have the same stuff. (T) (F)

11. Your life would be much better if you could have all the things you want. (T) (F)

12. Internet companies have asked you to fill out surveys and offer coupons so they can use that data to sell you more products. (T) (F)

13. When you buy something online ads will then pop up that seem similar. (T) (F)

14. Cookies on a website don't really get saved to your device. (T) (F)

BIG MONEY MISTAKES WE MAKE AS PARENTS AND GRANDPARENTS

As parents, we all want our kids to be well-adjusted, responsible adults who look back on their childhoods—and us—with fondness. None of us want our kids to be teased at school for their generic-brand sneakers or when they are adults, to have to worry about increasing credit card debt or how they are going to make the monthly mortgage payment. Sometimes, in our quest to give our kids happy childhoods, we send the wrong messages about money, which confuse our kids and harm the family's financial health. We all make mistakes, that's how we learn, and frankly, someone said; "Mistakes are proof that you are trying."

Here are some common mistakes parents (and grandparents) can make, and how you can avoid them.

Big Money Mistake #1: Believing That Your Kids (And Grandkids) Must Have What Other Kids Have

Giving our kids and grandkids what others have is pretty easy temptation. The desire probably goes back to your childhood. If you grew up having less than other kids or feeling that you did, then you don't want it to happen to your children. That's a large part of why you worked so hard to succeed.

But the answer to it is easy, too.

Is this a value you want your children to have? Do we want them to have a sense of entitlement? "I should have what those other kids have." "I have to keep up with the Joneses." Of course, we don't. You don't want to hint at the reality that you want them to impress their friends with possessions.

And the other sad truth is that some of their friends may be jealous of their things and hate them for that. The quote by Will Rogers puts it all in perspective; "Too many people spend money they haven't earned to buy things they don't want to impress people that they don't like."

I'm not saying that your kids can't have anything; I'm talking about balance.

Okay, it's tough on a kid to be the only one in school who's wearing nerdy sneakers instead of the latest Converse All Star Marvel Black Panther Comics high tops. And it's hard not to want to do something about that. But it's also tough to be the only kids with just one pair of cool Cons when everyone else has a pair for every day of the week, and it's tough to be the only one driving a used Toyota when everyone else has a new BMW.

And that, in a nutshell, is the main problem with keeping up with the Joneses. There is not a cut-off point. Once you're in that mindset, there is never enough. If the guy next door has the latest smartphone, then you won't be able to imagine being without the one that has the solar watch attached that can beam into space.

It's not attractive behavior, and we create kids that are never satisfied with what they have. It's not what we want for ourselves, and it's certainly not what we want for our kids. It will not bring you or them joy. True happiness will never be derived by trying to impress others. Richard Bach said, "I do not exist to impress the world. I exist to live my life in a way that will make me happy."

The solution: Stop and think. Ask yourself, "Why am I considering buying this for my kids or grandkids? Will it help them to do better in school? Will it add to their cultural enrichment? Will it help them develop the skills they need?

Or will it just add to their snob-appeal quotient?

There is nothing wrong with having nice things. But when kids get objects without realizing the amount of money they cost—and, therefore, the number of hours worked to earn them—there is a value disconnect that can start a cycle of wanting, and getting, more and more without ever really being satisfied.

Big Money Mistake #2: Shielding Your Teens From The Cost Of Things

One of the things that get us into trouble is the idea that you have to shield your kids from the harsh realities of money. "We don't want to take their childhoods away from them."

I've heard similar discussions from people who grew up in relatively comfortable households. "You just didn't talk about money. You didn't ask how much things cost. Polite people simply don't discuss it."

Anything that involves money, and exchange of value, can be used as a learning tool. Of course, you don't want your kids to ask the neighbor what he paid for his new lawnmower. But they can ask you. Explain that people, in general, don't like to discuss what they earn and spend and that a discussion with them may make them uncomfortable. But, if you are comfortable, discuss it with your kids. There is frankly no way for them to understand the cost of things until they know what things cost.

A good place to start is with a check in a restaurant. Ask them to figure out if it was calculated correctly (even if you perform the task with a calculator). It's a life skill to observe the table and know if the bill is correct. It's also a quick lesson in honesty. At some restaurants, the wait staff could have their paychecks docked for undercharging a patron. And then explain how to calculate a tip. Teaching the economics of being a waitress or waiter is a great life lesson, especially how much tips are part of their necessary income.

Have you ever seen a group of teens try to calculate a tip? Not a pretty sight. So, make this a family activity.

Shielding your kids from the cost of things can keep them from getting a good start. Keeping your kids in the dark will inflict unnecessary harm in the future due to financial ignorance. And sometimes, teens not only don't know how much things cost, but also don't realize that they—not their parents—may be responsible for the cost of repairing or replacing someone else's property should they damage it. Don't put your teen in that position.

Big Money Mistake #3: Using Credit To Buy Stuff For Your Teens When You Know You Shouldn't

The most significant financial danger to older teenagers—and college students especially—is the credit card. Youth, to whom the credit card is the most dangerous, are those who suffer from a value disconnect. They don't connect things with the money it costs to buy them; they don't connect money with the work hours it takes to earn it. When you spend money that you don't have to purchase something that your teenager wants—or even something your teenager needs—you may be thinking like Scarlett O'Hara, in *Gone With The Wind*, "I'll think about that tomorrow." When Scarlett did that, she was counting on herself to work, scheme, and improvise to come up with a way to get herself out of the jam. It frequently (though not always) worked for her, but that's Hollywood.

In real life, the message you are sending to your teenager is that you can buy things without worrying about how that purchase figured into your plan and how you were going to pay for them, and this is just about one of the worst messages you can send.

Big Money Mistake #4: Buying Something For Your Kids Because You Don't Want Your Ex (or the other grandparents) To Buy It For Your Kids

Kids have enough temptation to play divorced parents against each other, without putting more in their paths. And grandparents, if you are competing with the other set of in-laws, you know who you are. You are the ones who always come to the door bringing some wonderful gifts for your grandchildren. You want to be the cool grandparents.

You are who you are. If you are divorced, your ex is who he (or she) is, as well. If you couldn't change him (or her) when you were married, you are certainly not going to change them when you are divorced. If he's always wanted to be the big guy, buying the expensive things for the kids, don't compete with him for that role. It's the wrong competition, and it sends a very wrong message.

Divorce brings in a whole boatload of money problems, starting with the all-too-common huge disparity in income that may exist. Typically, a man's standard of living often goes up after a divorce; a woman's standard generally goes down. We all know why this happens. Many women drop out of the workforce to raise kids. Getting divorced also makes it harder to get back into a career that will pay you what you would have earned by not leaving the workforce. We also know that there is a gender gap in the workplace, with women only making 87 cents for every dollar a man earns. We also know this happens and how unfair the disparity is. But the point here is: How do we deal with it?

Here are the big issues.

Teens Playing Parents Against Each Other

It's laceratingly painful to hear your teen say, "I'm going to Dad's. He'll buy it for me. He'll let me do it."

It's a variation of "all the other kids' parents let them stay out till midnight" or "I'll be the only kid in my class who doesn't have pink hair—only worse." Worse because your teen can't move in with the cool, permissive parents down the block, but they may be old enough to move in with their other parent.

I've been stressing the importance of sending your kids clear, consistent messages about money management. So, what do you do when your ex has very different values from your own? As I mentioned before, if you have irreconcilable differences with your ex, there's not much chance that you'll be able to reason with him (or her). At this point, it'll be challenging to agree on values, even when it comes to something that should be a common concern, like child-rearing.

There was another time I had to counsel a couple on TV. I bring this up because they were the "poster children" for not only for teens playing parents off against each other, but for the kids being the pawns in the middle.

The father, in this case, had a very lucrative job. Mom was a lawyer who gave up her law practice to become a stay-at-home mom, leaving the workforce for 20 years. The stereotype continues...the husband, age 55, fell madly in love with his 25-year-old secretary, divorced his wife, and married the secretary.

The two children from the first marriage rebelled and refused to meet their new "stepmother" who was not much older than they were. Dad's reaction? He cut-off the funds to the kids (ages 18 and 23), who he was supporting. The kids panicked and approached Dad and said, "We will see the new wife if you reinstate our money." It got worse. Dad upped-the-bar with the manipulation and held the kid's economic hostage, saying he'd even pay them more if they stopped seeing their birth mother.

I sat them all down, off-camera to try to get them to see what was happening. I'm rarely at a loss. I was. The father said that it was his money, and these were the conditions. The kids wanted the money. I choked up, and the birth mother couldn't stop crying.

We went on air, and the audience was actually booing the father. He just smiled and said, "It's my money."

My reason for relating this tragedy is that money can be co-opted. The scene was about power. Money can be used as a destructive tool.

The only thing you can do is stick to your principles and values. When dealing with your ex, the only line that you can take is, "My house; My rules." Make sure that your values are consistent and that you feel right about them, and then stick to them.

What if your ex has a lot more money than you do and a more affluent lifestyle? There may be problems that you'd expect, such as your teen being seduced by the lure of affluence. And there may be problems you might not expect. You may need to reassure your teen that you are fine and that they needn't worry about you having less.

Be open with your teen or young adult about money and budgeting. If you take a matter-of-fact attitude about money, and you don't romanticize it or put it down, then you should be able to make your teen understand that just because you don't have a yacht, it doesn't mean you are a pitiful creature or a candidate for the poorhouse.

Big Money Mistake #5: Spending Money On Your Kids And Not Letting Your Partner Know

Most of us, for one reason or another, grow up being secretive about money, which is part of the story. The other part relates to the value disconnect. You may subconsciously feel that if you can hide it from someone, it didn't happen.

You know you don't want your kids to learn lessons of deception. And you don't want to put them in the position of conspiring with one parent against the other. But it can happen. It can get even worse if you bring the kids into the conspiracy, buying them things and telling them not to tell Mom or Dad.

You don't need me to suggest that it may be time to examine your behavior. However, I will suggest that you explain to your teens that you are aware of being a less-than-stellar role model. In this instance, adults make mistakes and also make poor choices. You are sorry and that you will try not to have it happen again.

Big Money Mistake #6: Spending Money On Your Kids And Not Letting Yourself Know

The cost of raising a child in 2020 will be $233,610.[28] A large chunk of that money will go toward housing your loved ones. But our under-25 age group of young adults and teens spend about $1,500[29] a year on clothing, and it seems that most of that money comes from parents. It's impossible to get a firm handle on the numbers, because as a parent or grandparent, you know, it's $20 here and $20 there. We hand money out in dribs and drabs without realizing it. You need to stop the flow and make sure that you communicate this to the kids. You are not the family ATM with unlimited privileges. Why teach the importance of earning and budgeting money if you are just going to undermine your system?

Big Money Mistake #7: Not Knowing What Your Kids Spend Their Money On

Do you need to know where your teen's money goes? Isn't that an invasion of privacy? The answer to this one is the answer to so many things: Use your good common sense. You don't have to make them account for every penny; that's not the point. But you should have a good general idea of their spending habits. That's why I recommend the Greenlight debit card. You will be able to see all of your child's purchases.

If you know what your kids spend their own money on, you'll know what they value. You'll know how they are changing, what kind of people they are becoming. You should know if your teen is spending too much...or perhaps hoarding too much.

You may be able to anticipate problems—or recognize some of them early on. A vital tip: Pay very close attention if your teenager starts to spend more money than they legitimately ought to have. This will probably be done in cash.

4 MONEY MISTAKES EVEN GOOD GRANDPARENTS MAKE WITH THEIR GRANDKIDS

Okay, grandparents, it's time to talk to you; alone. Think about your relationship with your grandparents. Were your memories about experiences with them or about the stuff that they bought you? I think you know the answer.

When I think about my grandparents, my Grandma Jewel showered me with unconditional love and was always there for me. Every Monday, she schlepped to our house and was waiting for me with a fresh roast beef sandwich on warm rye bread. We would sit and laugh and hug each other. She taught me her recipes, which I've passed to my kids. My matzoh balls are just as hard as hers! She was the only person (except for my Mom) who read everything I wrote and saw every TV show where I appeared. Even when I knew I had bombed (okay, so I once used a TV monitor as a mirror; on air; I fixed my make-up...live, or lost my shoulder pad on "The Oprah Show" in front of Stedman), Grandma Jewel was always there to tell me I was great and that all of her friends were watching. Arthur Kornhaber said it right; "If grandmothers hadn't existed, kids would have inevitably invented them."

My memories are about our relationship, not about the things she bought me. It will never be about stuff. When I worked at Chase Bank and David Rockefeller was our CEO, one day we were talking about possessions versus experiences, he told me; "You will never see a hearse with a luggage rack." He was right.

As a grandparent, I know that there is no greater joy than to experience the phenomenon of being a grandparent. Now, more than ever, grandparents are an incredibly important part of their grandchildren's lives. There are 65 million[30] grandparents in the US. Many of them are involved in raising our grandchildren.

Grandparents are an active part of the household. About 4.2 million households, or 3 percent of all households, contained both grandchildren under 18 and their grandparents in 2012. A grandparent maintained over 60 percent of these households, and about one in three had no parent present.

Whether or not you are raising your grandchildren, you have an incredible impact on them. Use this influence for good. It's not just about the money; it's about your caring conversation and actions. They are watching you and learning from you. Are you the grandparent you want to be when it comes to teaching your grandchildren about financial responsibility?

We are all trying hard. Grandparents, read these four money mistakes you're probably making and see if any resonate with you.

Big Money Mistake #1: *Not Preparing Your Kids And Grandkids For Their Inheritance*

We know that approximately $30 trillion[31] will transfer from our generation to our grandchildren. Because many baby boomers feel that their children have blown-it when it comes to money, much of the inheritance may skip a generation and head into their grandchildren's pockets.

I am not a believer that money should just magically transfer upon your death. Don't keep this secret; it sends the wrong message. You are not your money; you are your values. (I say that a lot because it is so important.) Let your grandkids know what is important to you and why you have left them this incredible gift. Tell them that their inheritance is not intended for them to drop out of school, lounge around the house, pierce and tattoo their body so they can live on a beach and not contribute to the world. (Okay, that judgment about tattoos and piercings may have come through; just sayin'.)

Convey to your grandkids what your dreams are for them. You may want to pay for college or to pay for their first home, or travel. Also, let your family know about your favorite charities and get them involved with those while you are alive. It's way more powerful to share your passions while you are there to explain their importance to you. There are even services that also let you record video messages to your loved ones after you pass. You know that it is too late, but it's a beautiful way to reinforce who you are and what your loved ones mean to you.

Big Money Mistake #2: Spoiling The Grandkids

Many grandparents may feel that "spoiling the grandkids" is part of the job description, but it's not. (Okay, I know that I just set myself up as the "evil money expert;" however, as a grandparent myself, you don't want to foster the, "I want, I want syndrome.") You may be the first to discuss your kid's parenting of the grandkids, citing that you think the grandkids are too materialistic and are frankly always asking for things.

Don't be surprised because you may have contributed to this pattern, creating a classic Pavlovian response, which leads to spoiling the grandkids. Do you always show up with a gift for the grandkids? You may think that this is the role of a grandparent, but it also fosters the "entitlement program," as I call it. You know how it works; Grandma or Grandpa show up, and the grandkids get a gift. When you don't, the first thing that grandkids may say is, "Where's my gift?" You may quietly think, "Wow these kids seem spoiled." Or, you may not be so silent and tell their parents. But, understand that you created this situation and these seemingly "spoiled" grandkids. They are only responding to your stimuli, just like Pavlov's dogs.

Build memories with your grandchildren. They want your time. You can do an activity with them. Do you cook or play golf? Those are great activities to do with the grandkids. You can turn all of these into learning as well. Cooking, for instance, involves reading a recipe or following Grandmas', a trip to the store to buy the ingredients, and then the science and art of making the dish. These activities can be simple; teach them to knit, or sew, or cook, or play a sport, or to play an instrument you play. Let them listen to your music, and you listen to theirs. I'm into making slime with my grandchildren. We are testing out all sorts of recipes. We also have "dance contests" jumping around to each other's music. I even did a TikTok with my granddaughter. Please don't search for it, we were in matching PJ's. Somehow, I never win the singing or dance contests, but the gales of laughter from my grandson at my "Hey Jude" rendition is worth it.

Big Money Mistake #3: Not Letting Grandkids Earn And Save Money

When you see that your grandchildren, regardless of age, are earning their own money and saving for something they have picked out as a goal...DO NOT undermine that empowerment by "surprising" them and buying it, thus preempting their quest. It sends just as wrong a message as trying to "out buy" the other set of grandparents. Maybe worse. Remember the first thing you saved your hard-earned money for? I bet you can still remember that Schwinn bike, or special lunch box. You felt empowered when you earned your money

1. **Leverage is**
   a. The gearshift in a car.
   b. The method the Egyptians used to move those humongous rocks to build the Pyramids.
   c. Debt

2. **Stock is**
   a. A base for soup.
   b. Large animals that Super Woman herds together and drives north to free them from the slaughterhouse.
   c. Part ownership in a corporation.

3. **Face value is**
   a. How you feel after an expensive facial.
   b. When you stand out on the sidewalk and stare directly at a diamond necklace in the window of Tiffany's.
   c. The value of a bond when it comes out or when it matures.

4. **A prospectus is**
   a. A date you found on Tinder.
   b. An old man with a white beard who wanders around the mountains leading a burro and looking for gold.
   c. A document explaining things about a company or mutual fund when they offer securities for sale.

5. **A mutual fund is**
   a. A party in a hot tub.
   b. Two people splitting the check at lunch.
   c. A company that invests money.

6. **Dollar-cost averaging is**
   a. Spending an extra fifty dollars on something you don't need to get a free item you don't want.
   b. Ten friends splitting the tab at lunch—one of them only had the salad and water.
   c. Investing a fixed amount in stock or mutual funds regularly.

7. **Diversification is**
   a. When two people get together to write a poem.
   b. Kim Kardashian's shoe closet.
   c. An investing principle that encourages you to buy different types of investments.

8. **A bond is**
   a. How you feel after eating too many bananas and rice.
   b. When your friend shares your political views.
   c. Debt that is issued by a government or a company.

9. **Laddering is**
   a. What you use if a kitten is stuck in a tree.
   b. A big run in your panty hose.
   c. A way to stagger the maturities of bonds or CDs.

10. **A load is**
   a. A pile of rocks.
   b. What you expect might be there when you say, "Honey, isn't your turn to change the baby's diaper?"
   c. A fee charged when you buy or sell mutual funds.

Difference Between Saving and Investing

They both help you to accumulate money. The FDIC insures savings accounts, and you will not lose your money, that's the good news. You should save your emergency money in your savings and have enough to transfer to your checking account to pay bills. Full stop.

Investments are the money you want to leave alone for the medium and long term. They are riskier, more volatile, and because the market could go down, you could lose your money. But, if you invest in some of the indexes, like the S&P or Dow Jones, although not guaranteed in any way, on average, over time, you should see returns. When you are young, you have time on your side, and your children can experience the miracle of compounding.

I love this quote from Warren Buffett; "I will tell you the secret to getting rich on Wall Street. You try to be greedy when others are fearful. And you try to be fearful when others are greedy." He is trying to be clever, and not saying, "Buy low and sell high." The other thing he left out is the time value of money and starting early.

I discussed this before, but just to drive the point home and to be as annoying as my kids say I am, I'll give you another example. If your child doesn't start investing until they are older, their money is simply not going to do the same work for them.

Facts: I love this and repeated it.

If you invest $2,000 a year (just $40 a week) for ten years at a 10% rate of return, starting when you're 21-years-old and stopping when you are 30, that $20,000 investment will have grown to over $985,000 by the time you reach sixty-five. Reread this one. You only invested $40 a week. That's a "fancy latte each day (something you won't even miss). But that missed coffee, or two pizzas or one dinner out a week, could have made you almost a millionaire at age sixty-five. Come on!

Okay, I'm on a roll. If you wait until you're 31-years-old and invest that same $2,000 a year for ten years at the same 10% rate of return, your $20,000 investment will be worth $400,000 by the time you reach age sixty-five.

Wait until you're 45-years-old and invest $2,000 a year for 21 years (until your retirement at 65), you will have invested $42,000, and your investment will be worth only $140,810.

You get the point.

Higher Education

Getting your kids to college is one of the greatest responsibilities and joys for any parent or grandparent. I believe that this is a gift that has life-time benefits. It will help to shape and influence everything about your child, who will use this time as their maturation and passport to adulthood. As Nelson Mandela said, "Education is the most powerful weapon which you can use to change the world."

All parents and grandparents, no matter how tight their financial pinch is, should do whatever they can to help out and advise their kids about how to make their dreams of an education a reality. More and more grandparents are also helping their grandchildren with college costs. As previously mentioned, we are seeing a new phenomenon when it now comes to the transfer of wealth. Because of the greater involvement by grandparents and the extreme costs of college, inheritance is going to the grandchildren to help with education costs.

Even though I believe that parents and grandparents should help their children to obtain higher education, by the same token, I believe that kids have to take responsibility for their college education, as well. I think this should be the case, even if the parents can afford to write a check for all college expenses. I recommend that you sit down with your child, way before they are ready for college and explain that you expect them to pay for some significant share of their college. I have left "significant" as a number that only you, as the parent, can choose. I believe that teens should be working during the summer and saving part of that money for their education. You may want to have them work and save for their spending money, or part of tuition, or housing, that is up to you. I find that kids are more engaged in college and more responsible when they have skin-in-the-game. If they are paying $5,000 a year toward their education, they may feel that blowing off that 8:00 AM class is taking money out of their own pocket.

College Costs Are Shocking

I'm not going to weigh in on whether you should encourage your child to go to college. I am a big believer in education and feel that not only is it worthwhile in and of itself, but it does often give young people a leg up when competing for jobs. And we know that pay scales increase with education levels. I guess that Benjamin Franklin said it the best; "An investment in knowledge pays the best interest."

But the harsh reality is that the costs surrounding a college education today are astounding. I remember trying to stay awake during my college orientation, where I was paying $1,500 in tuition a year in 1969 at The American University, and the President of the school said that our children could be paying ten times that. The audience of my peers guffawed at the absurdity of such a high increase. Boy, I wish he was right. I spent over 60 times that amount for my kids' college.

Today, the average annual cost of a four-year private college is $49,139.[34] And, public colleges cost, on average, $9,650 for in-state residents, and $24,930 for out-of-state residents. Before your high school student gets too far down the road getting their heart set on going to an expensive private college, you may have to sit them down and come clean if you have not saved enough to help them foot the bill, if that is the case. You all know the statistics about the staggering student loan debt; Americans owe over $1.67 trillion in student loan debt,[35] spread out among 44 million borrowers. That equates to about 70 percent of graduates holding debt obligations. To put this in perspective, that is about $620 billion more than the total US credit card debt. The Class of 2020 has to look forward to an average of $37,584 in student loan debt. The average student's monthly payment is approximately $350.

In the midst of this pandemic, with Gen Zers graduating into what they thought was a perfect job market, found their dreams dashed. Many of them were hired and fired before they could begin. Also, many Gen Zers are even questioning whether it was worth it or not to incur all of that debt and go to college in the first place.

I know it is tempting to want to be able to give your kids a debt-free education, but you need to remember that they are young and have lots of time to pay back any loans. They can borrow for their education; you can't borrow for retirement.

Saving For College - Here are some ways to consider saving for your child's education:

529 College Savings Plans – A 529 college savings plan operates in a way similar to an IRA or a 401(k) plan. That means that the government has allowed you to save for your child's or grandchild's higher education tax-free through several savings options; aggressive and conservative. These plans offer significant tax advantages allowing any gains to be tax-deferred. Once the funds pay for qualified expenses, the parents or grandparents will not pay federal taxes on your account's earnings, as well as the potential for state tax benefits. Your investment is tied to the stock market, so the account performance is not guaranteed and will fluctuate. Many people saw their 529 savings plummet during the 2008 recession, and if they needed the money for their college students, they didn't have time to regain their losses. For this reason, 529s allow the owner to alter the investments in the account. When the child is younger, and there are more years to "risk" the returns, you may want to invest in a more aggressive portfolio. As the college years approach and your offspring will need to withdraw the funds, you may consider a more conservative portfolio, making sure that the money saved is there when needed.

The 529 savings plan can be used for undergraduate or graduate studies at any accredited two or four-year college or vocational school in the U.S. If your child decides not to go to college, because you are the owner of the money, you can predesignate another child to be the recipient.

The other unique feature of 529s is that the proceeds can be used for tuition, books, fees, supplies, and room and board. You control the account; your child will not have access to it, and anyone can contribute to the account. I like 529s because they offer the most flexibility.

Prepaid Tuition Plans –

If you are confident that your child will attend an in-state public school, you may want to consider a prepaid tuition plan. Not all states offer these plans. Check to see if your state offers a program, and if available, you will pay for tuition credits at a predetermined price. Prepaid Tuition Plans provide the same tax advantages as 529's. Depending on your state's regulations, you may also get a state tax deduction. As noted above, 529 plans will fluctuate with the stock market, however, with prepaid plans, states may assume the market risk for the investor. In theory, the state guarantees plans, but there could be another risk when you read the fine print. In some cases, language may say that if the state and consequently, the plan is faced with a budgetary shortfall, investors could be in trouble.

The catch here is that if your child decides on another out-of-state school, you may not receive a reimbursement of the full value of your plan. It is also challenging for the states to keep up with the growing costs of college. The plan's investments could be growing at a slower rate that the costs of college. You can, as with 529s, change beneficiaries, but the money can only be used for tuition. If the funds are used for other expenses, a 10 percent penalty is applied.

Uniform Gift To Minors Act (UGMA) and *Uniform Transfer To Minors Act (UTMA) Accounts –*

As a parent or grandparent, you can set up an account in your name with your minor child as the beneficiary. The government rules allow you to make a financial gift to a minor (who will benefit eventually from the use of the money) and name someone as the custodian of that account. The first $1,000 (approximately) in gains is tax-free; the second $1,000 is taxed at the child's income tax rate (which is presumed to be lower than yours). The good news is that your child can use the money for any purpose when your young adult reaches the age of maturity (18 or 21, depending upon your state). The bad news is that your child can use the money for any purpose. If you have intended the money to go towards their college and they think that a Ferrari is what they want, it is often very hard legally to prevent that. Unlike the other college savings accounts above, you will not have the ability to transfer the account to another child or change beneficiaries when your child is eligible to receive the money.

The other bad news is that if your child is considering applying for Federal Financial Aid, a custodial account is viewed as an asset and will be counted against them.

Other Cost-Saving Alternatives

Coming up with cash is only one way for your teen to contribute to their education. They could "contribute" in other ways:

- ◆ *Community College*: Don't forget about your local schools. College-bound kids can start at a Community College. Last school year, the average tuition was approximately $4,891 for in-state students and $8,651 for out-of-state students; so, the savings can be significant. After a year or two of getting high grades, and hopefully meaningful internships during the summer, students can try to transfer to a private or state school to finish up their education. Also, their 2-year associate degree may open doors to any number of good-paying jobs. Some of those jobs may even offer your child further schooling as part of their benefits.

- *Summer Courses:* Your student can take summer courses and extra courses during the year to try to reduce their education to three years instead of four.

- *AP Courses/CLEP (College Level Examination Program):* They can take Advanced Placement courses in high school and try to get college credit for those, thus reducing the amount of required time and money to graduate. CLEP tests can allow you to reduce the number of classes you will have to take to graduate.

- *Grants/Scholarships:* There were approximately $3 billion[36] in unclaimed federal grant awards last year. Your child may fit the bill to be eligible to receive private grants and scholarships, as well. One or more of these can reduce your or their economic burden. They can speak with their high school guidance counselor or research grants and scholarships online. One popular one is a Pell Grant.

- *Vocational Schools:* Your child could show a special talent; cooking or selling real estate, or is a whiz at computer technology. Vocational schools offer a variety of courses. The average total cost of vocational schools in 2020 is estimated to be $33,000. That seems like a big price tag, except when you look at the total cost of a four-year private college, which will run you way over $127,000.

Borrowing Money

College is expensive, and there is no getting around that. Most students have to borrow to pay their way through school. If you and your children are going to go that route, they must understand their responsibilities when incurring debt. Student loans are a big responsibility and will become part of your young adults' budget for many years. As George Bernard Shaw said, "The surest way to ruin a man who doesn't know how to handle money is to give him some."

Student Loans can be federal or private. The U.S. Department of Education has two major federal student loan programs; The William D. Ford Federal Direct Loan Program, where the U.S. Department of Education is the lender and the Federal Perkins Loan Program, a school-based program. In 2020, the outstanding student loan debt reached $1.6 trillion and was owed by a collective of approximately 45 million borrowers. *Most Common Federal Student Loan Programs:* Stafford and Perkins loans are federal loans given directly to the student, often referred to as Title IV Funds. This government money carries low-interest rates and flexible repayment options. You or your child will not be required to have a credit check. The other positive point is that when they graduate, they can consolidate these loans to make the repayment-tracking process easier.

- ◆ *Most Common Private Student Loan Programs:* Sallie Mae operates as a private, publicly traded corporation and offers student loan options. Banks, Credit Unions, state agencies, and schools can also lend money. Private loans can supplement other financial aid or loans.

- ◆ *Private vs. Public Loans:* Many students turn to banks or credit unions to obtain loans. The difference between federal and private student loans is the cost and the use of credit scores in determining eligibility.

Here are some things to consider when applying for a public or private student loan:

	PUBLIC	PRIVATE
Interest Rates:	Fixed	Fixed
	Lower	Higher-dependent on FICO scores
Subsidization:	If needed	None
Repayment:	Flexible	Set schedule
	No repayment until graduation	May require payment during school
Loan Forgiveness:	If proven hardship	Harder to obtain
Co-signer:	Not needed	May need
Credit Check:	Not needed, in most cases	Usually required

Student Loan Debt

We know that this debt is crippling for many young adults. The standard repayment plans for federal student loans are estimated at ten years, but research shows that the average bachelor's degree holder takes 21 years to pay off their debt.[37] The Consumer Financial Protection Bureau, (CFPB) has indicated our kids are delinquent in repaying their obligations. There are many reasons for this, including the lenders not supplying the base level of service necessary to meet the borrowers' needs. Our kids are victims of misapplied or lost payments, amongst other mistakes. The CFPB says that 1-in-4 borrowers are delinquent or have defaulted on their student loan debt.[38]

If your students don't make payments on their student loan debt for more than 270 days, they will be in default.

They cannot ignore this. Student loans are considered forever-debt. There is no statute of limitations for federal student loans. Punto! (Keep reading, I deal with this later.) Even in bankruptcy, it's hard to have a student loan obligation discharged.

Parent Student Loan Debt

We love our kids. We will do anything for them to help make life easier, and we do. Taking on student loan debt for them is one way. Discover[39] conducted a survey and found that "61% (of parents) are very or somewhat likely to help (their kids) pay back loans. StudentLoanHero.com found that "55% of parents have more than $40,000 in student debt." Remember, these are both direct loans the parents took out, or loans the kids took out, on which the parents co-signed.

You can help to pay off your kid's student loan debt. That's generous, but you have to think of some consequences of doing that. The IRS[40] looks at that as a gift to your child. You can gift your child $15,000 (as of 2019) without incurring taxes. If you go over this amount, you, the donor, will pay the gift tax. It's frankly better to just pay the college bills directly. You can make unlimited, tax-free gifts of educational expenses instead of taking out more loans in your name or your child's.

Parent PLUS Loans are loans that are taken out by parents to pay for their children's education. They do come with a fairly high rate, now over 7 percent. As of the writing of this book, StudentLoanHero[41] notes that "there are over 3 million Parent PLUS loans with a total of $62 billion in debt. Please know that parents that use these loans are not eligible for income-based repayment or forgiveness, the way student loans are. In a word, you may be stuck.

Some Parent PLUS FAQs:

- **What is it?** A federally guaranteed parent loan that can be used to pay for your child's college.
- **How much can you borrow?** You can borrow each year, the full out-of-pocket cost of each child's annual college education.
- **Cost?** They are market-based and locked in. They are high.
- **How do you get one?** You call the financial aid office at your child's school and apply. But not everyone is accepted. You have to have good credit.
- **Bad news.** You are stuck with this debt, even in bankruptcy, because this is government debt.

Some 401(k) Borrowing FAQs:

Parents can also borrow against their 401(k)'s for college. (Pre-pandemic rules)

- **How much can you borrow?** If for whatever reason, parents cannot get a PLUS Loan, they can borrow up to $50,000 or half of the vested balance (whichever is less) for college.
- **You have to pay interest.** But technically, it is paid to yourself.
- **There is no real approval.** So, even if you have poor credit, you can get this loan.
- **It's not reported on your credit history.**
- **It has no effect on your student's ability for needs based (FAFSA).**
  But....
- **It is a short-term loan. These loans have to be repaid in 5 years.**
- **If you lose your job, you must repay it in 60 days.**
- **If it is not repaid, it will be treated as taxable income.** If you are under the age of 59 ½, this unpaid

amount will be penalized by an additional 10% early withdrawal fee.

- **You can't make new contributions until the loan is fully repaid.**

Some IRA Borrowing FAQs:

Parents can also borrow against their IRAs to pay for college, but the rules will make your head blow-off, so check them carefully. If you must use your retirement money, I'd rather have you use your IRA than your 401(k). Here are some things to think about:

- **The loans will reduce your funds for your retirement.**
- **If you take a distribution before age 59 ½, you are generally exempt from the 10% early withdrawal penalty.** The money must be paid to an eligible educational institution.
- **The funds have to be used for qualified expenses like tuition, fees, books, and room and board.**
- **If there is money left over, you can still use it for retirement.**

You may ask, "Are these kids helping to pay back these loans?" Well, StudentLoanHero.com[42] put that question in their survey, and almost "2 in 5 parents said their children never contribute to student loan repayment."

Sit Down Time:

Put your Big Girl Panties on and start the real discussion with your kids. Below are a few critical points:

- You can borrow for college; you can't borrow for retirement.

- Go over your child's budget (See No Magic Money Log on pg. 141) and show them how to structure repayment. You may agree to help and ease them into the monthly nut.
- Review to potentially consolidate and/or refinance loans.

What College Grads Need to Know About Their Student Loans

Make Your List And Check It Twice: Make sure your college graduate has a good list of all of the obligations that they have and are checking to see if their loans are federal or private. The distinction between federal and private loans is critical because different laws guide each loan structure, and any changes will not necessarily affect each of them in the same way. Grads need to note the interest rates on each loan and the terms and the grace periods before they have to start paying this back. For instance, a Stafford loan has a 6-month grace period before the first payment is due, but Perkins loans give a 9-month grace period.

National Student Loan Data System (NSLDA): This is the U.S. Department of Education's central database for student aid. They receive information from schools and other education programs and provide a centralized view of Title IV loans and grants, so if your child is a recipient, they can access data and make inquires. Your child can glance at their data and make sure that it is correct. They have to also keep the data up to date. If your grad has moved, they must notify the NSLDA. If your child thinks that they are going to have a problem paying back their loans, it is critical to communicate that situation to the NSLDA. *Unemployment Or Hardship:* If your children have federal student loans and are unemployed, they may be granted temporary forbearance on their student loans. They would have to qualify for an income-based repayment plan, however. There is also a Pay-As-You-Earn Plan, and this, too, can cap loan repayments if they are eligible. There are other programs, but your youth would have to inquire about not only the plans but their qualifications to obtain these. You or they can inquire about federal loan repayment plans by visiting: studentloans.gov/repay.

Continuing Education: In some cases, if grads have a federal loan, and they decide to enroll for an advanced degree, they may be able to obtain a deferment on their student loans.

Note: Forbearance means a delay in loan repayments; however, the interest will still accrue.

Defaulting. Make sure that your grad understands an event of default. According to the Department of Education, one in four student loan borrowers' default on their loans. For a loan made under the William D. Ford Federal Direct Loan Program or the Federal Family Education Loan Program, your child will be in default if they don't make their scheduled student loan payments for about nine months. For a loan made under the Federal Perkins Loan Program, you are considered in default if you don't make any scheduled payment by the due date.

Develop Your Repayment Plan. Your grad needs to build this debt repayment into their monthly budget. It is tough for this loan to disappear, albeit, there are reasons for your student loans to be forgiven, but it is not easy. I will not cover this in great detail, but in a Chapter 7 bankruptcy petition, there are cases for discharge, but "undue hardship" has to be proven.

Living on your own is not just different from living at home; it's *a lot different,* even if prepared. Without planning, it can be *shockingly* different.

What should your teenager be paying for--- and what bills should you pay? To what extent should your teen be involved with managing their budget?

The teen years are the dress rehearsal for real life. We all have a burning parental desire to shield our children, guard them against pain and suffering, and protect them from the harsh realities of life. But by the time they're teens, some of the harsh realities of life are there, and the others are just around the corner. And there's no better anchor for a teenager than learning to take financial responsibility.

You are still responsible for your kids' basic needs---shelter, food, clothing, and education. Even so, opportunities to teach your kids how to manage money do exist.

The Bill-Paying Game

For younger teens not exposed to the concept of household budgeting, I have developed a "game" to show them how your real budget works visually. If you haven't shown your kids real bills; real life, it's time to consider this. Sit down with your kids and show them how your paycheck is deposited automatically and how you get notified. You will have to feel comfortable with this process. Next, you will lay out all of the bills. Start with the first deduction, which we know is taxes. Ask your kids to count out your tax bill applicable for that pay period. You have to explain your tax-bracket and the percentage that they have to figure out. Obviously, with teens, you are just going to show them your monthly statements and don't have to make this a game.

Take the next largest bill, which is probably your mortgage or rent. Again, they count out the money. You get the point. Add all of your expenses like car payments, gas, utilities, cell plans, phone bills, cable, health and life insurance, food, clothing, savings for college and retirement, charity, entertainment, emergency money, etc. Make sure that you do not scare the kids if you happen to fall short each month. The exercise is supposed to be enlightening and instructive. If it's more comfortable doing this online, the impact will not be dramatic, but they will understand the lesson in budgeting.

You can point out that with each category, there are "needs" and "wants" that can significantly influence any budget. For instance, food is a necessity, but designer coffee and juices can increase the food budget.

Teens tend to assume that they will make a lot more money than they actually will, especially in their early years, so a realistic discussion of income and expenses is in order. For the most part, children tend to shy away from lectures. They may, however, like to hear stories about your first apartment, how you found it, how you furnished it, and what it cost per month and how you paid for it.

Start With Training Wheels: Clothing

Like food, clothing can be a necessity or a luxury---and a shared responsibility. The challenge here, as just mentioned, is that teens not only think they'll make more money than they will, they also tend to believe that things cost less than they do. As such, teens make purchasing decisions by the designer label, rather than the price tag.

And that's all right. There's nothing wrong with having good taste or developing your taste. But teens need to know what items cost, and how much more certain objects cost than others. We want them to start thinking in terms of: How many hours of work would it take to afford the designer jeans? That is the real value.

My daughter, Kyle, was on Oprah's show with me. She wasn't a teen yet, but close. Oprah asked her what her goal was for her Medium-Term Savings. Kyle quipped, "Originally, my goal was to buy a pair of awesome designer jeans." Oprah asked her if she was wearing them on-air that day. Kyle sort of shrugged and flashed me a look and said, "I decided not to buy the jeans because it was going to take me twenty weeks of work to afford them." Unfortunately, Oprah made her turn around to see if there was a designer label. The look on Kyle's face was not good. She was mortified as she showed her butt with a generic pair of jeans. I don't think she even heard the audience break out in their ovation.

You are responsible for making sure that your teen has clothes that fit, that are warm in the winter and cool in the summer, that are dressy for weddings and simple for funerals. You want to make sure they have clothes appropriate for college and job interviews, and casual ones for hiking or working out. You are not responsible for making sure that they have designer labels.

One of the best ways to handle the development of teenage responsibility in budgeting, spending, and decision making is right here.

Sit down with your teen each quarter to figure out a budget. First, allow them to make their list of all the items they think are necessary. They have to include everything from coats to socks to sports equipment. They then have to research the costs of each item and add up the total. You may be shocked, and they may also be shocked. Then, you review the list and cull it down to a reasonable amount for your budget. Perhaps three pairs of designer jeans are not what you are willing to buy, but maybe you will spring for two pairs of generic jeans, instead.

I realize that this process is tedious, but it is a lesson in reality and budgeting. The rules are that they can earn the extra money to make up the shortfall if they so choose. You need to explain the rules upfront. Allowance for clothing is being given for a specific period, in this case, for three months. The agreed amount of money could be in the form of a debit card, which your teen will have to manage. This process will involve some real decision making. If they mess up, they will learn from that. Try not to fill in the gaps. I promise that the next quarter – if you stick to your guns – will turn out better.

Debit Card

A debit card issued by a bank allows you to transfer money electronically to another bank when you make a purchase. Debit cards eliminate the carrying of cash. The money is deducted from your checking account. In theory, you can't overdraw your account, so your child will have a finite amount of funds loaded on their debit card to spend. Debit and credit cards look the same. The difference is that a debit card takes the money from your bank checking account, and a credit card charges it to your line of credit and thus creates a loan that carries interest.

Several debit cards give parents the ability to "look over your teens' shoulder" to view their spending habits. I'm in favor of that control. Let your teen know that this is the type of card you are getting. In some cases, the cards allow teens to shop in certain places, will not permit cash withdrawals, and even "greenlight" purchases by you before completing the transaction. Look into the various options to see what is right for you and your child. As mentioned, I work with a company called, Greenlight. I elected to work with them because we share our values around educating kids to be responsible with money. Their debit card allows kids to have the freedom to spend while also having the parents decide on the acceptable places for kids to shop and spend.

Getting Your Teens And Young Adults Involved In Your Budget

You have shown your kids your real budget. It's a perfect time to encourage them to have constructive input. They can create their own ideas for *budget-hacks*. Maybe they can research ideas to bundle internet and TV services and save you money? They can come up with ideas for other cost-cutting categories, as well. Do they have suggestions for carpooling, or buying in bulk, or cooking and freezing meals each week? If you challenge them, I bet they will be creative while learning how a real family budget works, before they are responsible for their own.

Getting College Students On A Budget

I have talked a lot about the teenage years as a dress rehearsal for real life, and the college years as halfway into the real thing.

Your kids are still your kids. They aren't earning their own living and starting families yet—but they aren't living at home, under your roof, anymore. Your day-to-day connection with them is going to change. This generation of parents and grandparents is way more involved than was mine. We were just dropped off at school and knew that if we didn't have any money, we couldn't spend it and couldn't hit our parents up for any, either. I worked my way through college and paid for everything myself. But frankly, in my day, we could. Kids today can't.

I'm also in favor of keeping close tabs on your teen's budget process when your child goes to college. The budget will slowly be expanded to include more items; however, the process of a three-month or even a month-to-month basis is best until you are comfortable with your young adult perhaps managing their first real budget.

You Need To Know Where You Have Been Before You Can Decide Where You Want To Go

If the budget process is new to your teen, it is vital to take a step back at this point and help them to assess where they have been before they can set goals as to where they are going. I have created a simple process called, the *No Magic Money Log.* Based upon the simple theory that every penny of your teen's money gets spent on something, the *No Magic Money Log help teens* keep a record of everything they spend.

I find it easier to go low-tech with this, but if your teen wants to use their smartphone, that is perfect. I like to carry a small spiral memo pad or small file cards. Every day they will record everything they spent, no matter how inconsequential. There is no "miscellaneous" category. Within a short time, maybe a week or a month, they will have a reviewable record that will tell them exactly where all of their money goes. It is step one in any money-management plan.

No Magic Money Log

Day of Week:
Amount Spent:
Item Bought:
Need or Want:
Planned or Impulse:

My Fir$t For Teens

The teen years may be the first your child is exposed to the financial tools they will need to obtain and manage. In this section, I will go through some of those basic tools, how to get them, and special features of each that your teen should consider.

Bank Accounts:

--Checking: In today's digital world, it's almost unnecessary to use a brick-and-mortar bank; in fact, most young people will prefer online banking as a convenience. Online banking provides the use of bank services via the Internet. Your teen will be able to deposit money online or through the mail, pay bills, transfer money to others or between their accounts, and receive ATM privileges to access cash. Your teen needs to compare fees for each bank because they all will not charge the same rates.

--Savings: A savings account is one of the simplest types of bank accounts. Your teen can temporarily store cash securely while earning interest. Banks and credit unions each offer savings accounts. A savings account is the perfect financial vehicle if your teen is saving for a purchase, such as a car or college, and will have to pay for these in the short term. Again, your teen needs to check the fees and interest rates. Note, I have said "temporarily" stored, because the interest rates paid on savings accounts are very low, and there are better alternatives if your teen is saving for the long term (a year or more). Typically, online savings accounts at credit unions pay higher interest rates than big banks.

There are three types of standard savings accounts:

--Basic Savings Account: An account where your teen deposits their money and can withdraw it at any time. It's perfect to have emergency money kept in this type

of account. Ideally enough to cover a three to six-month emergency fund should be kept on hand. In the case of your teen or young adult, a $500 account should cover any unexpected emergencies and give them a cushion.

--Money Market: A money market account often requires a higher balance than a checking or savings account, to be kept and usually pays a slightly higher rate. Sometimes this account has check-writing and debit card privileges. Usually, transactions are limited to a handful each month.

--Certificate Of Deposit (CD): A CD is when you put money into a savings account for a fixed term, anywhere from a few months to a few years. Again, because you are committing your money for a longer-term, the financial institution will pay a slightly higher rate than other types of savings accounts.

All these bank accounts are covered by the Federal Deposit Insurance Corporation (FDIC), an independent agency of the U.S. government. The FDIC insures the depositor for their principal plus interest owed up to $250,000 in any one bank. Credit unions have similar insurance through the National Credit Union Insurance Fund (NCUSIF).

License To Drive

Even the concept of having your teen drive will make you upset. Really upset. It's really about their safety. Teens are careless and think they are invincible. My greatest nightmare is of the "Terrible Ts:" Texting and Teens. It's real and scary. There was a sign outside a church that read: "Honk if you love Jesus. Text while driving if you want to meet him." It's funny, but it's not. According to the National Safety Council, 1.6 million car accidents are caused each year due to texting.[43] And according to USA Today, 43% of teens text while driving.[44]

Your teen may have permission to drive your car, which comes with a whole host of responsibilities and costs. It was Erma Bombeck who said, "Never lend your car to anyone to whom you have given birth." That is a good rule, but not realistic.

Every teen wants a car—right? Buying a car could be their first foray into the world of finance, in a big way. They may think that they can afford a car if they only save enough money to buy that $4,000 old clunker. They need to think again. Have your teen research all of the costs involved in buying, owning, and operating a car.

The list should start with the cost of the car, new or used. Many websites can help with the car researching process. Their list also has to include all of the other costs associated with that car, which should consist of insurance, maintenance, and gas.

Speaking of car insurance, hopefully, your teen's research will explain why male teen insurance premiums are more expensive than a similar policy for a female of the same age. The average 18-year-old male will pay almost $3,000 a year, while his twin sister will pay $1,500 a year. Also, let your teen compare their premiums if placed on your policy. The costs should be lower. Their research should include not only if they are going to buy a car, but also if they are going to drive yours. Premiums are also affected by where you live, what type of car you drive, and if you have been a responsible driver. Teens may negotiate reduced insurance rates by maintaining good grades.

Activity: Teens will create a budget to buy and maintain a car.

Goal: To allow your teens to learn about the budget process around something they want, like a car.

(Note: I do not want to introduce the concept of leasing a car. I want to keep this first foray into budgeting as simple as possible.)

Instructions: Read this with your teen or discuss this in your own words:

You are going to build a budget to buy a car. You can research the costs of vehicles online. You have to decide whether you are purchasing a new or used car. You have to consider all the expenses involved each year to buy the car, drive it, and plan for unexpected events. You are trying to figure out what you would have to earn (before you paid all of your taxes) to support that car. Pretend that you only have to worry about the car; you are not worried about living anywhere or buying food or clothes. The challenge is only to figure out how much you have to earn to purchase and maintain the car. We have done the math for you.

Scenario 1: You buy a second hand or new economy car. Research the different costs involved in the purchase. (The following are some expenses your kids should consider. They will have to estimate real yearly costs based upon their research.)

ECONOMY CAR EXAMPLE:

Cost to buy: $18,000
(Assume your child obtained a car loan for four years with a 10% interest rate, payable equally over the 4 years.)

Cost of the car = $18,000 ÷ 4 = $4,500 in principle payments per year
10% Interest: $4,500 x 10% = $450 per year
$4,500 + 10% Interest = $4,950 that they have to pay per year

More: Challenge your kids to think of all of the other things they have to consider that will cost money. Here is a list to use, after they have shared their ideas. They have to research each estimated cost and figure that in. It's a great time to discuss how young men will pay more for insurance than young women. Ask your teen why they think that is the case? (Answer: Young men statistically are a greater risk, and the insurance companies have to pay out more money because they have more accidents than young women.)Challenge your kids to think of all of the other things they have to consider that will cost money. Here is a list to use, after they have shared their ideas. They have to research each estimated cost and figure that in. It's a great time to discuss how young men will pay more for insurance than young women. Ask your teen why they think that is the case? (Answer: Young men statistically are a greater risk, and the insurance companies have to pay out more money because they have more accidents than young women.)

Example:

Cost of car per year	$4,950
Insurance Premium	1,200
Maintenance (car wash, oil, etc.)	500
Gas (15 gallons per week at $3.00/gal)	2,340
License Fees/Inspection (not Annual) + misc	300
Total Yearly Cost	**$9,290**

Challenge: *(Ask your teen) How much would you have to earn each year just to cover your expenses on your car? Assume a 30% tax bracket.*

Formula: 1. Subtract the difference of 30% from 100%
       (1 -.3 = .7)
    2. Divide the yearly cost by .7
       ($9,290 ÷ .7 = $13,272)

Answer: **They would have to earn $13,272 each year just to cover the expenses of $9,290 for their car.**

Scenario 2: Now you want to buy an expensive luxury car. Again, the goal is to figure out how much you will have to earn each year to afford the car of your dreams.

LUXURY CAR EXAMPLE:

Cost to buy: $80,000
(Assume your child got a car loan for four years with a 10% interest rate, payable equally over the 4 years.)

Cost of the car = $80,000 ÷ 4 = $20,000 in principle per year
10% Interest: $20,000 x 10% = $2,000 per year
$20,000 + 10% Interest = $22,000

Example:

Cost of car per year	$22,000
Insurance Premium	4,000
(Explain that this is higher because it costs more to fix an expensive car.)	
Maintenance (car wash, oil, etc.)	2,000
(It's more costly to maintain a luxury vehicle.)	
Gas (15 gallons per week at $3.00/gal)	4,160
(More powerful engines consume more gas and need Premium gas.)	
License Fees/Inspection (not Annual) + misc	300
Total Yearly Cost	**$32,460**

Challenge: *(Ask your teen) How much would they have to earn each year just to cover their expenses on this car? Assume a 30% tax bracket.*

Formula: 1. Subtract the difference of 30% from 100%
$(1 - .3 = .7)$
2. Divide the yearly cost by .7
$(\$32,460 \div .7 = \$46,371)$

Answer: **They would have to earn $46,371 each year to cover the expenses of $32,460 for this car.**

Note: Many people lease a luxury car, and they do not have to fully pay for the cost of the car in the lease. You can also have your child research the price of a lease and how it works after they understand this preliminary exercise. This activity is only appropriate for more advanced conversations, because your child must have a good credit rating to get a lease, and would probably not qualify without you co-signing the lease.

Other Games To Play With Your Younger Teens

Everybody wants something, and we can confuse a want with a need at any age. Giving teens some control over their expenses may highlight the difference between *need* and *want*. Play the *Need vs. Want* game while you and the kids are in the car together, and you have a captive audience – their ideas may surprise you! The whole family can play *Need vs. Want*. The younger kids will begin to catch on and want to play this over and over again. Call out items on a list and ask each person to decide whether the item is a *need* or a *want*. The older kids may start to say things like, "You need shoes, but you don't need designer shoes." That's when you know this exercise is working!

WHICH IS IT? NEED OR WANT		
Shoes	○ NEED	○ WANT
Jacket	○ NEED	○ WANT
Haircut	○ NEED	○ WANT
Ice Cream	○ NEED	○ WANT
Smart Phone	○ NEED	○ WANT
Premium TV Subscription	○ NEED	○ WANT
Laptop Computer	○ NEED	○ WANT
Car	○ NEED	○ WANT
Car Insurance	○ NEED	○ WANT

YOU MAY NOT HAVE TO WORRY ABOUT THE EMPTY NEST SYNDROME

Today's Millennial or even Gen Z children may not be able to make ends meet financially, and they may be moving back home with Mom and Dad or even with Grandma and Grandpa. According to Zillow,[45] as the pandemic struck, as of March and April of 2020, there were 32 million adult children who moved back into their parents or grandparents home. It was the highest number on record. More than 80% of those who recently moved back in with their elders are Gen Zers. Some of these kids are helping out with sick parents or grandparents, as well.

In many cases some of these young adults and Millennials are part of the gig economy who suffered great layoffs during the pandemic. Frankly, this trend is almost entirely due to the pandemic; but another reason is their vast student debt burden. The other phenomena are that even though technically we are pulling out of the new recession, and jobs are more plentiful, your Gen Z child may not be able to find a high paying job, right-off-the-bat.

If your grown offspring (temporarily) fails at the American Dream and must choose between going from friend to friend or living in your home, we are parents and grandparents first, and the door is always open. In today's world, it's better to just think of our young adults as *free-range kids*.

There is hardly anyone I know who could say no to a child who needed to move back home. You are their rock. Kobe Bryant said, "My parents are my backbone. Still are. They're the only group that will support you if you score zero or you score 40." That is the major issue, but you still need to address specific guidelines to ensure that this boomerang situation will be more workable. You may be in a time of your life where you were budgeting to have your expenses reduced or you may have down-sizing plans in mind because you didn't need the large family nest anymore.

The other thing to consider is not to assume that things will pick up the way they were when your child went to college and returned on vacations and summers to work. Everything has changed. Your child has changed, you have changed, and the world has changed. It's not easy to accept the fact that this parent-child situation can ever go back to the way it was, it can't; it won't.

Avoid the situation where you become, "Hotel Mom and Dad," that comes replete with room service and gas in the car. Having your grown children at home can be a great time to teach or reinforce some of the imparted wisdom. You gave them roots, and you gave them wings. You love them. You just may now think about having; "a talk."

I recommend that you have a conversation about house rules and responsibilities. I'm not being harsh; it is your house. Misunderstandings can take place, and those can lead to tough times; for you all. Expectations also need to be explicitly discussed and memorialized. When I say, "memorialized," I mean written down in a lease. You do not have to have a lease drawn up by a lawyer; you are a family held together by love and trust. But this has to be taken seriously.

Why Draw Up A Lease Between Parent And Adult Children?

The point of the lease is to lay out the rules that you both agree upon so that you lessen the friction or unpleasantness later on. Whether your offspring chooses to stay in or return to the nest, an agreement establishes them as an adult. You now recognize them as an adult with certain freedoms and responsibilities.

Your child may welcome an agreement that lays out what their obligations are because it reduces feelings of dependence and helplessness. Even if your youngster cannot share the full financial burden of running a household, they can help with physical chores that could have great value to you.

Here are some guidelines on what should be addressed in this lease. Most of the points are financial and have no right or wrong answers. The process is to facilitate open and frank conversation. If there are personal issues, you know what they are and add them, as well. Things like a time limit on how long the child stays under a parent's roof and who pays for what will differ significantly from family to family.

How To Set Up A Lease With Your Adult Child

The lease discussion should start at the point when your young adult has decided to wait before leaving home, or before they move back into your home. It is much harder to break old habits after your child has established residency. Don't wait for the first blow-up. This will all seem punitive; you want it to be generative.

Remember, in this case, you are the landlord, and the child is the tenant. While you want to relate to your offspring as an adult, you do have certain prerogatives that the child does not.

Below is a brief list of questions that you, as a landlord, need to ask yourself and your partner first to establish what you feel is fair to request of your child. These questions focus on the trouble areas that generally come up in a household. Many of these points actually would be addressed in an apartment lease, so it is not unreasonable for you, as a landlord, to focus on them.

1. Should your adult child pay rent? Yes ____ No ____

2. How much rent should your child pay?
    $ ____ if employed; $ ____ if unemployed

3. Should the lease be for a specific time period?
    Yes ____ No ____

4. How do you divide utilities? Go bill by bill and
    be specific.

5. What household chores are the responsibility of
    your child? Be specific and include outdoor and
    indoor duties.

6. Is your child allowed to use your car?
   Who pays for gas, maintenance, and insurance?

7. Is your child allowed to have pets? Who takes care
   of them and pays for those expenses?

8. May your child eat your groceries, or do they have
   to shop for their own? Who makes the food list?
   Who buys the food?

9. Who prepares the meals, and what is the
   schedule?

10. Does your child need assistance in setting up a
    workable budget, taking all obligations, such as
    student loan debt, car expenses, health insurance,
    etc., into account?

The above questions do not constitute a quiz; there are no right or wrong answers. It is a conversation starter to help you and your child to frame an open discussion around this new living situation. You all will decide what goes into the "lease," including, if you want to memorialize it in writing (which I recommend). Every family can address additional subjects, such as smokers versus nonsmokers, entertaining guests (when and where), party privileges, etc.

The next step is to write out the lease with the mutual decisions you all feel are fair and appropriate. As always, you are willing to negotiate. For instance, perhaps your offspring would be willing to take on the responsibility of car maintenance for the privilege of parking their vehicle in the garage.

Note: The lease discussion might serve as a great conversation starter for a child who is planning to move in with a roommate. They will have similar questions and need to work these out before moving in together.

THE IMPORTANCE OF INSURANCE

Why is there so much talk about insurance? Because unexpected things can happen to us, our loved ones, or our possessions. These occurrences can not only hit us emotionally, but also cost us lots of money. Simply put, people buy insurance to protect themselves from losing money in the future, caused by an event that may happen. You are trying to cover yourself for an unpredictable accident or death or disaster.

The truth is that you can, for enough money, insure anything. Lloyds of London, an insurance company in the UK, has been insuring almost anything since 1688.

Some of my favorite policies are:

- Leg insurance. Heidi Klum got her legs insured by Lloyds of London for $2,000,000. And, the policy was issued to Proctor & Gamble, who hired her as a spokesperson. Here is the kicker (no pun intended); one leg was insured for more than the other because one was valued at about half of the other because it had a tiny scar on it.
- Injury by falling coconut insurance. Yup, in 1984, it was shown that about 150 people died a year from falling coconuts. And yes, there were pay-outs.
- Hair insurance. Yes, from Tom Jones' chest hair to Santa's beard to Pro-football players' lock, Lloyds has insured them.
- Abduction by alien's insurance. Over 20,000 people, including Shirley MacLaine, took out alien abduction insurance.

- Breasts. Dolly Parton had insured her breasts for $600,000.
- Body. David Beckham, the international soccer star, had his body insured for $195,000,000.
- Fingers. Keith Richards had just his guitar-pick-holding middle finger insured for $1,600,000. And Jeff Beck insured each one of his fingers for $1,000,000 each.
- Voice. Bruce Springsteen had his voice insured for $6,000,000.

Types of Insurance

Life Insurance – Paid to a beneficiary (the person getting the money) at the time of death of another person. The purpose is to provide protection to your family or loved ones in case you die. Your kids may be too young to support themselves, or your partner may not have enough money to live without you.

How much insurance do you need? I want you to figure the number out for yourself. You need to know how old your kids are and how long you want to support them if you are not here. You need to ask yourself questions like the ones below and put a real cost by each one:

- Do I want my kids to live in this house? How much will that cost (mortgage, utilities, repairs, and for how many years?
- Do I want to provide for college? Private or public?
- Will the kids be going to public or private school now?
- Are the kids going to summer camp or taking vacations?
- Is there childcare for the kids?

You get the point. You will need to have enough insurance to cover all of these costs for as long as you want to provide a particular lifestyle for your kids.

My biggest cautionary note is that most people are under-insured and think that because they are young, this is a decision you can push off...don't do that.

Property Insurance – This is exactly that insurance against anything happening to your property, like your home, boat, or car. You want to be protected from accidents, damage, fire, theft, etc.

Liability Insurance – This insurance protects you if someone gets injured by you or because of you or on your property. You want to safeguard yourself from legal damages or legal costs. Auto liability insurance will protect you if you are found at fault in a car accident and someone is injured. It will also pay for the cost of any damages to the vehicles.

No-Fault Auto Insurance – Many states offer this type of insurance. Broadly, you and the parties involved are indemnified for losses regardless of the accident and whose fault it is.

Health Insurance – This is insurance that covers the whole or part of medical expenses for you and your family.

When looking into insurance, you need to consult professionals to see what suits your needs and your pocketbook. Before you speak to a professional, who wants to sell you a policy, think about what you are trying to achieve and who you want to protect. If your adult child has lost their job, it's really important that they have health insurance. The pandemic has really highlighted this situation. Currently, they can stay on parents' insurance until they are 26 years old. They can do this, even if they; get married; have or adopt a child; start or leave school; live in or out of their parents' home; aren't claimed as a tax dependent; or turn down an offer of job-based insurance coverage.

How to talk to your young kids about insurance

The big question that I have found with kids is that they want to know, "What happens to them if something happens to you?" You don't want to scare your kids, but a throw-away line, like, "Don't worry, you are taken care of" is insufficient. That doesn't explain a thing and just pushes them off from asking other questions.

Let's face it, we live in a world of the internet, a world of instant information. Our kids know about every disaster. They know about terrorism, floods, accidents, illness, and other horrors of life, and COVID-19, resulting in death. Even our fairy tales point out horrible things.

We are raising our kids, reading about the princesses whose mothers or parents died, only to be raised by the evil step-mother. Or cute cartoons where Bambi's mom gets shot in the first few minutes or *Lady and the Tramp* orphaned immediately, or *Lion King*, where the father dies suddenly. Or how about in *Frozen*, where a shipwreck leads to the death of Elsa and Anna's parents, and where Kristoff is also an orphan. Let's add *Peter Pan* to the list, where the Lost Boys have no parents; or *Aladdin* where Jasmine's mother is dead, and Aladdin is an orphan, called a "Street Rat." Add *Pocahontas* to the list where the mothers and sometimes fathers are absent or dead. In *Lilo & Stitch,* Lilo and Nani's parents died in a car accident. In the *Rescuers*, Penny has no parents. And, let's not forget *Star Wars*, where there is a dead mom and an absentee dad with the Skywalker children being raised by relatives. I have to stop researching this; I'm crying and frankly upset that we have been raising our kids with this fairytale tragedy.

Our kids are bombarded with this every day, and you need to address their fears. You will reassure a 5-year-old differently than your 15-year-old. Try to be as honest as possible.

Your 5-year-old wants to know 5-year-old information, like; where will they live if something happens to one of you; will they stay in the same school? Will they still go to summer camp? Will they go to live with an aunt or uncle?

With the 15-year-old, it's time to sit down with them to lay out the financial situation. Will they live in the same house? Will they get a car? Will there be money for college? With your older young adult children, they need to know exactly what happens to them, and also what your wishes are, as well. These are really uncomfortable conversations, but you need to have them. Make it as easy as you can for your kids. Lay out all of the necessary paperwork, contact numbers of the legal, accounting, insurance, financial advisors and other important people in your life. Your discomfort will allow them some comfort. It is a gift to your kids.

THE END

The fact is that it's not the end. You are watching your baby turn into a toddler, who turns into a preschooler, who morphs into a teenager and grows up to leave the nest (and may return). Have you given them good advice? What do you still need to do?

As long as you are alive, you are a parent, and hopefully, -- you will keep on parenting...and grandparenting. You should keep asking yourself, "What are all the things that I wish someone had told me when I was my kids' age?" That will guide you. And the other guiding question is: "Does it matter profoundly?"

When you reflect upon the question "What is this all about?" I think it's all about you as parents and grandparents giving the gift of self-reliance to your kids...even in tough times. Never lose track of that goal and reinforce it. Self-reliance builds self-esteem. Self-reliance paves the road to financial freedom. My book is supposed to be - just a guide. I want to help you navigate through each of these phases so you can be the parent you want to be. Here is the good news. We all make mistakes. We are human. But the big take away is that we love our children and grandchildren unconditionally. That is their anchor...and that love is our anchor.

What do you still absolutely have to, positively need to do?

Give your kids a kiss.

Trust yourself...Trust your kids.

Thank you for allowing me to be your guide. Visit me at www.NealeGodfrey.com.

Index

Endnotes

1   "Americans Feeling More Financially Secure, But Many Significantly Underestimate Healthcare Costs, Life Insurance Needs and Longevity, Financial Engines Study Shows," *Bloomberg*, September 7, 2017, https://www.bloomberg.com/press-releases/2017-09-07/americans-feeling-more-financially-secure-but-many-significantly-underestimate-healthcare-costs-life-insurance-needs-and.

2   "National Financial Literacy Test Results," *National Financial Educators Council*, https://www.financialeducatorscouncil.org/national-financial-literacy-test.

3   "Student Loan Debt Statistics in 2021: A Look at The Numbers," *Student Loan Planner*, updated January 19, 2021, https://www.studentloanplanner.com/student-loan-debt-statistics-average-student-loan-debt.

4   "Charge-Off and Delinquency Rates on Loans and Leases at Commercial Banks," *Board of Governors of the Federal Reserve System*, last modified September 30, 2020, https://www.federalreserve.gov/releases/chargeoff/delallsa.htm.

5   "Parent Student Loans Survey: How Do They Affect Parents and Their Debt?," *Student Loan Hero by LendingTree*, March 13, 2018, https://studentloanhero.com/featured/parent-student-loans-survey/

6   "A Look at the Shocking Student Loan Debt Statistics for 2020," *Student Loan Hero by LendingTree*, last modified January 15, 2020, https://studentloanhero.com/student-loan-debt-statistics.

7   Richard Fry, "For First Time in Modern Era, Living With Parents Edges Out Other Living Arrangements for 18- to 34-Year-Olds," *Pew Research Center*, May 24, 2016, https://www.pewsocialtrends.org/2016/05/24/for-first-time-in-modern-era-living-with-parents-edges-out-other-living-arrangements-for-18-to-34-year-olds.

8   Jonelle Marte, "U.S. household debt tops $14 trillion and reaches new record," *Reuters*, February 11, 2020, https://

www.reuters.com/article/us-usa-fed-household-debt/u-s-house-hold-debt-tops-14-trillion-and-reaches-new-record-idUSKB-N20521Z.

9   "Big-Picture Thinking Leads to the Right Money Mind-set," *Capital One*, January 27, 2020, https://www.capitalone.com/about/newsroom/mind-over-money-survey.

10   NEFE/The Harris Poll, "Nearly 9 in 10 Say COVID-19 Cri-sis is Causing Financial Stress," *National Endowment for Financial Education® (NEFE®)*, April 16, 2020, https://www.nefe.org/news/2020/04/survey-covid-19-crisisi-causing-financial-stress.aspx.

11   "Divorce Statistics: Over 115 Studies, Facts and Rates for 2020," Wilkenson & Finkbeiner, Family Law Attorneys. https://www.wf-lawyers.com/divorce-statistics-and-facts/

12   Linda Gallo, PhD, "Speaking of Psychology: The stress of money," *American Psychological Association*, March 2015, https://www.apa.org/research/action/speaking-of-psychology/finan-cial-stress.

13   "Survey: Certified Divorce Financial Analyst® (CDFA®) professionals Reveal the Leading Causes of Divorce," *Institute for Divorce Financial Analysts*, https://institutedfa.com/Lead-ing-Causes-Divorce.

14   "Women of Working Age," *U.S. Department of Labor*, https://www.dol.gov/agencies/wb/data/latest-annual-data/work-ing-women.

15   Consumer and Community Development Research Section of the Federal Reserve Board's Division of Consumer and Community Affairs (DCCA), "Report on the Economic Well-Be-ing of U.S. Households in 2015," *Board of Governors of the Federal Reserve System*, May 2016, https://www.federalreserve.gov/2015-report-economic-well-being-us-households-201605.pdf.

16   Monique Morrissey, "The State of American Retire-ment," *Economic Policy Institute*, March 3, 2016, https://www.epi.org/publication/retirement-in-america/#charts.

17   Stan Higgins, "From $900 to $20,000: Bitcoin's Historic

2017 Price Run Revisited," *CoinDesk*, last modified December 17, 2020, https://www.coindesk.com/900-20000-bitcoins-historic-2017-price-run-revisited

18   "Lifetime Effects: The High/Scope Perry Preschool Study Through age 40." Ypsilanti, MI: High/Scope Educational Research Foundation, 2005.

19   "IRI Baby Boomer Expectations for Retirement 2017," *Insured Retirement Institute*, April 5, 2017. https://irionline.org/research-and-education/reports-and-factsheets-page-2.html

20   "Millennials Are Lousy Savers, but Their Parents Were Worse," *Bloomberg*, November 20, 2014. https://www.bloomberg.com/news/articles/2014-11-20/millennials-are-lousy-savers-but-baby-boomers-were-worse

21   Bob Pisani, "Baby boomers face retirement crisis — little savings, high health costs and unrealistic expectations," *CNBC*, last modified April 9, 2019. https://www.cnbc.com/2019/04/09/baby-boomers-face-retirement-crisis-little-savings-high-health-costs-and-unrealistic-expectations.html

22   Federal Reserve Bank of New York, Research and Statistics Group, "Quarterly Report on Household Debt and Credit," *Federal Reserve Bank of New York*, November 2020. https://www.newyorkfed.org/medialibrary/interactives/householdcredit/data/pdf/HHDC_2020Q3.pdf

23   Cameron Huddleston, "Survey: 69% of Americans Have Less Than $1,000 in Savings," *GOBankingRates*, December 16, 2019, https://www.gobankingrates.com/saving-money/savings-advice/americans-have-less-than-1000-in-savings

24   Liz Hamel, Cailey Muñana, and Mollyann Brodie, "LA Times Survey Of Adults With Employer-Sponsored Health Insurance," *Kaiser Family Foundation*, May 2019. http://files.kff.org/attachment/Report-KFF-LA-Times-Survey-of-Adults-with-Employer-Sponsored-Health-Insurance

25   "Consumer credit reports: A study of medical and non-medical collections," *Consumer Financial Protection Bureau*, December 2014. https://files.consumerfinance.gov/f/201412_cfpb_reports_consumer-credit-medical-and-non-medical-collections.pdf

26   Center for Microeconomic Data, "Household Debt and Credit Report (Q3 2020)," *Federal Reserve Bank of New York*, September 30, 2020. https://www.newyorkfed.org/microeconomics/hhdc.html

27   Jenn Jones, "Average Car Payment: Loan Statistics 2020," *Lending Tree*, January 8, 2020. https://www.lendingtree.com/auto/debt-statistics

28   Mark Lino, "The Cost of Raising a Child," *U.S. Department of Agriculture*, February 18, 2020. https://www.usda.gov/media/blog/2017/01/13/cost-raising-child

29   Ann C. Foster, "Consumer expenditures vary by age," *U.S. Bureau of Labor Statistics*, December 2015. https://www.bls.gov/opub/btn/volume-4/consumer-expenditures-vary-by-age.htm

30   "10 Percent of Grandparents Live With a Grandchild, Census Bureau Reports," *United States Census Bureau*, October 22, 2014. https://www.census.gov/newsroom/press-releases/2014/cb14-194.html

31   Anna Robaton, "Preparing for the $30 trillion great wealth transfer," *CNBC*, November 30, 2016. https://www.cnbc.com/2016/11/29/preparing-for-the-30-trillion-great-wealth-transfer.html

32   "What Percent of Americans Own Stocks?" *Financial Samurai*, https://www.financialsamurai.com/what-percent-of-americans-own-stocks/

33   J.B. Maverick, "What Is the Average Annual Return for the S&P 500," *Investopedia*, updated February 19, 2020. https://www.investopedia.com/ask/answers/042415/what-average-annual-return-sp-500.asp

34   "Tuition costs of colleges and universities." *National Center for Education Statistics*, 2019. https://nces.ed.gov/fastfacts/display.asp?id=76

35   Travis Hornsby, "Student Loan Debt Statistics in 2021: A Look at The Numbers," *Student Loan Planner*, updated January 19, 2021. https://www.studentloanplanner.com/student-loan-

debt-statistics-average-student-loan-debt

36   Medha Imam, "$2.9 billion unused federal grant awards in last academic year," *USA Today*, January 20, 2015. https://www.usatoday.com/story/college/2015/01/20/29-billion-unused-federal-grant-awards-in-last-academic-year/37399897

37   Jarrett Skorup, "The Student Debt Problem is Widely Misunderstood – Here Are Some Solutions," *Mackinac Center for Public Policy*, October 24, 2019. https://www.mackinac.org/the-student-debt-problem-is-widely-misunderstood-here-are-some-solutions

38   "CFPB Concerned About Widespread Servicing Failures Reported by Student Loan Borrowers," *Consumer Financial Protection Bureau*, September 29, 2015. https://www.consumerfinance.gov/about-us/newsroom/cfpb-concerned-about-widespread-servicing-failures-reported-by-student-loan-borrowers/

39   "More Students Expected to Help Pay for College as Parents Become Less Worried about Costs," *Discover*, May 9, 2016. https://investorrelations.discover.com/newsroom/press-releases/press-release-details/2016/More-Students-Expected-to-Help-Pay-for-College-as-Parents-Become-Less-Worried-about-Costs/default.aspx

40   "Frequently Asked Questions on Gift Taxes," *Internal Revenue Service*, updated November 9, 2020. https://www.irs.gov/businesses/small-businesses-self-employed/frequently-asked-questions-on-gift-taxes

41   Melanie Lockert, "Top Lenders to Consolidate and Refinance Parent PLUS Loans," *Student Loan Hero by LendingTree*, June 4, 2020. https://studentloanhero.com/featured/top-banks-consolidate-refinance-parent-plus-loans/

42   Andrew Josuweit, "Our Top Picks for Student Loan Refinancing," *Student Loan Hero by LendingTree*, October 10, 2019. https://studentloanhero.com/best-banks-to-refinance-your-student-loans-lendingtree-003

43   Taylor Covington, "Texting and Driving Statistics," *TheZebra.com*, updated January 28, 2021. https://www.thezebra.com/resources/research/texting-and-driving-statistics

44   Nikola Djurkovic, "24 Texting and Driving Statistics (Updated for 2020)," *CarInsurance.net*, January 29, 2020. https:// carsurance.net/blog/texting-and-driving-statistics

45   "$726 Million in Rent at Risk as Gen Z Moves Back in with Parents During the Coronavirus," *Zillow*, June 11, 2020. http://zillow.mediaroom.com/2020-06-11-726-Million-in-Rent-at-Risk-as-Gen-Z-Moves-Back-in-with-Parents-During-the-Coronavirus-Pandemic

NEALE GODFREY

Neale S. Godfrey is the financial voice for women and multi-generations and a world-renowned speaker and author, who has inspired millions through her work. She motivates, trains, educates, and frankly, entertains by delivering her core message: Empower yourself to take control of your financial life.

As the creator for the topic of "kids and money" and the preeminent thought leader for family financial literacy, Neale Godfrey has worked tirelessly over the last 35 years to connect the family around the topic of money.

In 1972, Neale began her journey as one of the first female executives at The Chase Manhattan Bank (the world's largest bank at the time). She later became President of The First Women's Bank and founder of The First Children's Bank in FAO Schwarz. Neale was also involved with the Institute for Youth Entrepreneurship in Harlem.

In 1989, Neale formed her own company, Children's Financial Network, Inc., with the mission of educating children and their parents about money. An author of 28 books empowering kids and their parents to have a healthy relationship with money, Neale is most recognized as The New York Times #1 Best-Selling Author of *Money Doesn't Grow on Trees: A Parent's Guide to Raising Financially Responsible Children.*

Among her many accomplishments, Neale developed the first money curricula for children and young adults, Pre-K through High School, *The One and Only Common Sense/ Cents Series,* as well as an interactive computer game called *MoneyTown.* More recently, Neale partnered with Tom Hester (Character Designer of Shrek) to give a facelift to her money characters. Those characters are featured in all three of Neale's #1 Educational mobile gaming apps in the App Store.

Neale has represented global companies as a National Spokesperson; including Microsoft, UPS, Lincoln Financial, Fidelity, AIG, Nuveen, Aetna, Coca-Cola, among others. She has also appeared as a financial expert on programs such as; *The Oprah Winfrey Show, Good Morning America,* and *The Today Show,* on major news networks such as; CNN, CNBC, and FOX Business, and starred in the PBS Special, *"Your Money, Your Children, Your Life."* Neale is also a popular contributor for Kiplinger, a former contributor to Forbes.com and Huffington Post, and a former Nationally Syndicated Columnist for the Associated Press.

Neale has served on White House and Governor's Task Forces, as well as on the Board of Directors of UNICEF, UNWomen, Young President's Organization — YPO (Member since 1987), The NY Board of Trade, and Morris County Chamber of Commerce. Today, Neale serves the following organizations on their Board of Advisors: Greenlight Financial

Technology, Inc., a debit card and investment platform for children, giving parents the ability to "greenlight" transactions; DriveWealth, LLC, a registered broker/dealer with a mobile investing platform; EarlyBird, an app for parents, family, and friends to make financial gifts to kids; and the National Urban League Guild, an auxiliary volunteer group that supports the National Urban League and affiliates across the country.

She is also an Executive in Residence and Innovation Fellow at Columbia Graduate School of Business and the Senior Mentor for the *Think Bigger: The Innovation Method* course. Neale is a popular contributor for Kiplinger, a former contributor to Forbes.com and Huffington Post, and a former Nationally Syndicated Columnist for the Associated Press.

Neale works intensively with Wounded Warriors as a faculty member of Veteran Women Igniting the Spirit of Entrepreneurship (V-WISE), and Entrepreneurship Bootcamp for Veterans with Disabilities (EBV), which are both operated by The Institute For Veterans and Military Families at The Whitman School of Management of Syracuse University.

As a leader in the financial literacy space, Neale has earned recognition from the White House for her program, *LIFE, INC: The Ultimate Career Guide for Young People*, sponsored by Deloitte Foundation, and honored with awards such as:

- Woman of the Year
- Banker of the Year
- Muriel Siebert Lifetime Achievement Award (for her trailblazing work on financial literacy) • NJBIZ Best 50 Women in Business Award
- Child Advocate of the Year - Femme Award of Excellence, UNWomen
- National Winner, w2wlink's Ascendancy Awards for Business Women

- Garden State Woman of the Year
- Awarded for Outstanding Service Toward Financial Literacy, United Negro College Fund • Women of Influence Award, Commerce and Industry Association of New Jersey
- National Honoree, WomenInBusiness.org

Neale Godfrey graduated cum laude from The School of International Service at The American University.

Despite all of her achievements, her kids and grandkids find it really cool that she was an answer on Jeopardy! as well as a question in The New York Times crossword puzzle.